THE WAR
THAT NEVER
ENDED

Pocket Essentials by Gordon Kerr

THE WAR THAT NEVER ENDED

A SHORT HISTORY OF THE KOREAN WAR

GORDON KERR

Oldcastle Books

First published in 2020 by
Pocket Essentials, an imprint of
Oldcastle Books,
Harpenden, UK
www.pocketessentials.com

Editor: Nick Rennison

A CIP catalogue record for this book is available from the British Library.

ISBN
978-0-85730-388-2 (print)
978-0-85730-389-9 (ebook)

2 4 6 8 10 9 7 5 3 1

Typeset in 13pt Adobe Garamond Pro
by Avocet Typeset, Bideford, Devon, EX39 2BP

Printed and bound in Great Britain by Clays Ltd, Elcograf S.p.A.

For Lindsey and Sean

CONTENTS

CONTENTS

Glossary of Acronyms

DMZ – the Korean Demilitarised Zone (a strip of land running across the Korean peninsula that acts as a buffer zone between North Korea and South Korea)

DPRK – Democratic People's Republic of Korea (North Korea)

ECA – Economic Cooperation Administration (the agency set up by the US Government to administer the Marshall Plan)

JCS – Joint Chiefs of Staff (a committee of senior United States armed forces leaders that advises the president of the United States on military matters)

MDL – Military Demarcation Line (the land border line between North Korea and South Korea)

NKPA – North Korean People's Army

POW – Prisoner of War

ROK – Republic of Korea (South Korea)

UN – United Nations

UNC – United Nations Coalition

UNCOK – United Nations Commission on Korea

UNTCOK – United Nations Temporary Commission on Korea

USSR – Union of Soviet Socialist Republics (the Soviet Union)

VJ Day – Victory Over Japan Day (the day on which Japan surrendered in World War II)

Introduction

The Korean War is the war that never ended, a conflict between two parts of what was once one nation, the Republic of South Korea and the Democratic People's Republic of Korea. But it was also more than that. It began in 1950 and was a war between two systems – the capitalism of the West and the communism of Russia, a front in the Cold War that was fought in the aftermath of the Second World War.

However, in comparison to other modern conflicts, the Korean War seems strangely neglected, probably most familiar to people through the hugely successful television comedy series *M.A.S.H.* And yet, it was a costly war. The United Nations force that supported South Korea after it was invaded by North Korea lost more than 178,000 troops, with 32,925 listed as missing and more than half a million wounded. North Korea suffered up to half a million dead and almost 700,000 were wounded. A staggering 2.5 million civilians lost their lives during the conflict. Three times as many British troops perished in the Korean War as in the Falklands War and the Chinese probably lost hundreds of thousands of soldiers, although the actual number remains uncertain.

It heralded a dangerous time in global relations and only the Cuban Missile Crisis of 1962 created a greater risk of nuclear warfare in the years since 1945. It was also the only conflict since 1945 in which two of the world's superpowers confronted each other in battle.

Perhaps it is the fact that it ended in a kind of stalemate, preventing any of the participants from bathing in the glory that victory engenders, that has made us neglect it over the years. Nonetheless, it was a significant event in modern history and featured a dazzling array of political and military talent – names on the Western side such as US President Harry S Truman, Secretary of State, Dean Acheson, and Generals Marshall, MacArthur, Ridgway and Bradley. On the side of the DPRK were the North Korean leader, Kim Il-sung (1912-94), grandfather of the current leader, Kim Jong-un, the Chinese leader, Mao Zedong (1893-1976), the Chinese Prime Minister Zhou Enlai (1898-1976) and the General Secretary of the Russian Communist Party, Joseph Stalin. The war itself featured significant military events such as the defence of the Pusan (now Busan) Perimeter, the destruction of the inexperienced and inadequately supplied US force known as Task Force Smith, the surprise landing of UN troops at Inchon (now Incheon), the advance of UN forces as far as the Yalu River on the Chinese border and the surprise Chinese intervention in October 1950.

As in the disastrous Vietnam War of a decade and a half later, for which the Korean War could almost be said to have been a dress rehearsal, the difficulties of sustaining an unpopular, autocratic government and of sending a modern, Western army to fight in difficult terrain against a lightly equipped, fast-moving and committed enemy soon became apparent. Eventually, by the time the armistice was signed at Panmunjom in July 1953, the Western Allies were happy to end their involvement in a costly and fairly thankless conflict in which victory for either side was impossible.

The War That Never Ended follows the events that led to and created the conflict and then guides the reader through the political machinations, personalities and battles of this brutal war. At a moment when North Korea is a hot topic, due to the efforts of US President Donald Trump to negate its nuclear capability, this book provides a timely examination of the events in the Korean peninsula that helped to shape our world.

1

Land of the Morning Calm

The Korean Peninsula

The mountainous land of Korea, nicknamed in English 'Land of the Morning Calm', stretches 600 miles from north-east to south-east and measures about 150 miles across at its widest, narrowing to under 100 miles between Pyongyang in the west and Wonsan in the east. To the north, it is separated from Manchuria by the Yalu and the Tumen Rivers and there is a tiny, 11-mile border with Russia at the mouth of the Tumen. The terrain is rough and the weather extreme – temperatures range from 40 to -40 degrees Celsius – and both these factors make operations difficult for a Western mechanised army. The mountains reach 9,000 feet and the countryside consists mainly of sinuous, narrow valleys punctuated by rice paddies and terraces.

Legend has it that the god-king, Dangun, founded Gojoseon in the northern part of the Korean peninsula in 2333BC. Gojoseon endured until 108BC when it was conquered by the Chinese Han dynasty which set up four commanderies. These were annexed by the Korean kingdom of Goguryeo and, by 313BC, Goguryeo was in control of most of the peninsula and the southern and central parts of Manchuria.

The medieval Goryeo dynasty – from which Korea derives its modern name – was established in 918AD. Its capital was originally at Kaesong but was later moved to Seoul, with the country remaining a tributary state of China. Despite a series of invasions by the Mongols, Goryeo was never conquered, but swore allegiance to the invaders. Eventually, when the Yuan dynasty in Mongolia began to crumble, Goryeo was free to re-establish its independence. The Yi dynasty came to power in 1392 and ruled the country until the Japanese annexation of 1910, but the families who ruled the country constantly engaged in feuds and Korea still looked to China as its 'elder brother nation'.

Korea existed in virtual isolation until 1876, when a Japanese military expedition arrived and, after some resistance from the Koreans, persuaded them to sign a treaty that opened Korean ports to Japanese shipping and gave rights in Korea to Japanese citizens. Thus, Korea was taken out of the Chinese sphere of influence. In 1882, the Koreans signed a treaty of 'amity and commerce' with the United States, infuriating the Japanese who now made efforts to become even more involved in Korean affairs. The British, meanwhile, were eager to counter Russian influence in the Far East by encouraging Korea to maintain its relationship with China. Japanese ambitions, however, were to make Korea 'a part of the Japanese map'.

In 1894, the Japanese seized the initiative, landing an invasion force, leading the panicked Korean government to plead for help from the Chinese. By the time they did so, Japanese troops were already in the capital. By 1896, the Korean king had sought refuge in the Russian embassy, and the Japanese were in full control of the country. But, when the king issued an order that all his pro-Japanese ministers should be executed, the Japanese backed down. Only temporarily, however.

For the following seven years, Korea was a bone of contention between Moscow and Tokyo as each vied for power and influence. In February 1904, following the breakdown of negotiations, Japan launched a surprise attack on the Russian Far East Fleet in Port Arthur (now Lüshunkou District) in China, followed by staged landings in Korea. In May, Japanese ships destroyed the Russian fleet in the Tsushima Strait, forcing the Russians to sue for peace and Korea was declared a Japanese protectorate in November 1905. At the time, the British were happy to recognise Japan's move in return for Tokyo's support for British rule in India.

The Koreans looked on in horror as Japanese bureaucrats and officials took over their entire country. Japanese roads and railways were built and Japanese education was introduced. Resistance grew and, by

1908, a guerrilla army 70,000 strong had lined up against the occupiers. The Japanese introduced harsh repressive measures that brought mass executions and imprisonment, gradually wearing down resistance. Finally, in 1910, the last Korean emperor, Sunjong (1874-1926), was forced to abdicate and Korea was formally annexed by Japan. Military government was imposed and for the next 35 years, the Japanese ruled in Korea, using the peninsula in the 1930s as a base from which to launch operations in Manchuria. They remained hated and there was continued resistance by nationalists in the mountains, many of whom were communists. In 1919, 7,000 peaceful Korean demonstrators were killed by Japanese police and soldiers.

In 1943, at a conference of the Allies in Cairo, President Franklin D Roosevelt, Prime Minister Winston Churchill and Generalissimo Chiang Kai-shek declared their commitment to a unified and independent Korea after the hostilities ended. They sought a trusteeship by the major powers, the United States, the USSR, China and Great Britain. However, at the later Potsdam Conference, it was concluded that there should be some kind of dividing line between the operations of the Americans and the Russians. The Americans decided unilaterally that they required two ports in Korea and the line they proposed should be drawn north of Seoul, therefore including the ports of Inchon on the west coast and Pusan on the east coast.

At the end of the war, Japanese forces north of the

38th Parallel were ordered to surrender to the Russian forces and those south of the line to US forces. It is worth pointing out how arbitrary the 38th Parallel was. It cut through provinces, towns and villages, and it cut off the more heavily industrialised north from the predominantly agricultural south. Of course, it was hard for one part of the country to survive without the other. In terms of numbers, around 21 million lived south of the Parallel and the remaining 9 million lived north of it.

The Russians accepted the American plan for division of Korea at the 38th Parallel and they stopped their advance into the peninsula at that point, about a month before the Americans were able to get troops there. It is actually debatable whether the United States would have put up much of a fight if the Soviets had decided to continue past the 38th Parallel and occupy the entire peninsula because Korea appeared at the time to have no real value. But Stalin was happy to settle for just a bit of it and China, for its part, was preoccupied with its own internal struggles, ignoring what was happening to the south.

America Takes Control

Towards the end of August 1945, troops of XXIV Corps were dispatched to Korea. Little was known about their mission, although their commander, General John R Hodge (1893-1963), was informed by a superior that the occupation was to be 'semi-friendly'. The Supreme Commander for the Allied Powers in Japan, General Douglas MacArthur, made it clear that the Koreans should be treated as a 'liberated people'. Washington ordered Hodge to 'create a government in harmony with US policies'. What those policies were, was a mystery to all, however. Hodge, therefore, ordered his men to treat Korea as an enemy of the United States which should be subject to the terms of the Japanese surrender. He gave himself the mandate of seizing power in Korea and controlling the country, refusing to have dealings with any Korean with a political position in order to maintain a distance between the United States and any of the various political factions in Korea. Initially, however, the Americans had to rely on the Japanese colonial officials, whom General Hodge immediately confirmed in their positions. Japanese remained the main language by which the Americans communicated with officialdom. On 11 September, however, MacArthur ordered that the Japanese had to leave immediately.

In the next four months, 70,000 Japanese bureaucrats and more than 600,000 Japanese soldiers and civilians were sent home. For the Koreans, however, it was a little too late as the initial good relations between the Americans and the Japanese had antagonised them, and they felt the Americans had treated them with contempt. This feeling was exacerbated by the fact that many of the Koreans who replaced the Japanese officials had been long-term collaborators with the Japanese and, as a result, were hated by their fellow countrymen.

Before their departure, the Japanese made it clear to the Americans that amongst Korean political parties, communism was becoming hugely influential, this at a time when the United States was becoming increasingly wary of the communist threat around the world. Hodge was anxious, therefore, to support political groupings that were anti-communist. The most obvious of these was the Korean People's Republic Party, whose members were nationalists and part of the anti-Japanese resistance.

In March 1946, the Joint Commission, representing the USSR and the United States, met and almost immediately was deadlocked over who should govern a united Korea. The Russians would only countenance the Korean communists and the Americans, of course, opted for the parties of the right. This led to each occupying power deciding to establish Korean states in their own respective zones. The USA assembled the South Korean Interim Government, dominated by a right-wing coalition led by Syngman Rhee (1875-1965). Americans remained heavily involved in an advisory capacity and retained control over financial matters. Meanwhile, in the north, in early 1946, a national Provisional People's Committee, with Kim Il-sung at the helm, came to power. Later in the year all the North Korean political parties were grouped into the Korean National Democratic Front and, in November, this body won 97 per cent of the votes in elections for new people's committees which led to the creation of the Korean People's Assembly.

The Joint Commission met once more in May 1947, and was greeted by violent protests. The Americans and the Soviets each put forward a proposal, the Americans seeking free elections for the whole peninsula, the Russians countering with a plan for an assembly with equal representation from both the American sector and their own. After each side rejected the other's proposal, the issue of Korea was handed over to the United Nations which created the Temporary Commission on Korea – known as UNTCOK – to oversee elections. However, the nations in the Soviet sphere of influence boycotted the vote and the Russians refused to allow the Commission access to the north of the peninsula. Nonetheless, on 10 May 1948, elections – regarded as illegal by the Soviets – were held in the south, the conservatives winning most seats. Three months later, on 15 August, the Republic of Korea was proclaimed, with Syngman Rhee as its president. Meanwhile, on 3 September, a new constitution was ratified in the north by the Supreme People's Democratic Assembly and a week later Kim Il-sung became Premier of the new Democratic People's Republic of Korea.

In December 1948, the United Nations designated South Korea as the only Korean state based on 'the free will of the electorate' and established a UN Commission on Korea. The ROK was recognised by the United Kingdom, Canada, France and the United States but neither Korean state was admitted to the United Nations.

Syngman Rhee

Born in 1875, son of a genealogical scholar, Syngman Rhee converted to Christianity in 1894 and studied English before becoming a journalist while earning extra cash by teaching Korean to Americans. He became involved in anti-Japanese politics and was imprisoned in 1899 for his involvement in a plot to remove King Gojong (r.1897-1907) from power. Released in 1904, he emigrated to the United States where he became active on behalf of Korea, meeting with Secretary of State John Hay (1838-1905), and President Theodore Roosevelt (1858-1919) in an effort to persuade the United States to help the cause of Korean independence. Rhee remained in America, earning a BA from George Washington University and an MA from Harvard. He also gained a PhD from Princeton. He returned to Korea in 1910 but was implicated two years later in a plot to assassinate the Japanese Governor-General of the country and was arrested. He managed to flee to the United States shortly after.

His exile in the United States lasted 35 years, spent lobbying on behalf of his beloved country's independence, his work paid for by donations from like-minded Koreans. Some thought that Rhee was too preoccupied with self-promotion, while some considered him to be arrogant. Others distrusted him for not participating in the armed struggle in Korea. But his determination was undeniable. Even other expatriate parties agitating, like him, for Korean independence, fell foul of him. He had a single-minded vision of the world and its future and would not be distracted from that. In 1944, when the United States still believed that it could co-exist harmoniously with Stalin's Soviet Union in a post-war world, Rhee was arguing that, 'the only possibility of avoiding the ultimate conflict between the United States and the Soviet Union was 'to build up all democratic, non-communist elements wherever possible'.

Rhee's grasp of English and his knowledge of America and American institutions gave him a real advantage over his rivals. Moreover, he was free from any suspicion of collaboration with the Japanese. He was obsessive and uncompromising in his nationalist and anti-communist sentiments and was emerging, in the minds of the American government after the war, as a possible future leader of his country.

2

Invasion

The NKPA Crosses the 38th Parallel

At 4am on the morning of 25 June 1950, the North Korean People's Army (NKPA) launched an invasion of the Republic of Korea. An artillery barrage in a number of locations was swiftly followed by the crossing of the 38th Parallel, on a front 150 miles wide, by seven infantry divisions and an armoured brigade as well as a number of other units. Alongside this force were 150 powerful Russian-built T-34 tanks. The invading army was around 90,000 strong and it was opposed by four ROK divisions and a brigade, all poorly equipped.

The Ongjin peninsula in the north-west was quickly taken as the offensive proceeded from west to east and by 9.30 that morning, the city of Kaesong (now in North Korea) had fallen. The main force began to proceed along the Uijongbu corridor – a route taken centuries earlier by invaders from Mongolia and Manchuria – that led directly to the capital, Seoul. In the central, mountainous region, the city of Chunchon (now Chuncheon) was threatened by two divisions and on the east coast in Gangwon-do province, there were amphibious landings at Gangneung and Samcheok. Attacks by North Korean, Russian-built Yakovlev Yak-9 fighters were launched on railway stations, airfields and petrol storage tanks in Seoul.

At 11am, North Korean radio announced that the North Korean government had declared war on South Korea in retaliation for an invasion of the country by what it described as 'the bandit traitor Syngman Rhee'. North Korean Premier, Kim Il-sung, reiterated this version of events on North Korean radio at 1.55pm and by 3pm on the first day of the conflict, North Korea was claiming that its forces had penetrated 10 to 15 miles into its southern neighbour.

It took three hours for the news of the invasion to reach the US Far East Command headquarters in Tokyo, in a message from the American Embassy military attaché in Seoul. There was great surprise in the South Korean capital, as well as in Tokyo and Washington. Of course, they were fully aware in these places that the North Koreans were entirely capable of launching an invasion, but the notion had hitherto been discounted.

Meanwhile, on 26 June, as the North Koreans continued their advance southwards, the United Nations Commission on Korea (UNCOK) passed the following conclusions to UN Secretary-General Trygve Lie (1896-1968):

'Commission's present view on basis this evidence is first that, judging from actual progress of operations, Northern regime is carrying out well planned, concerted and full-scale invasion of South Korea; second, that the South Korean forces were deployed on wholly defensive basis in all sectors of the parallel; and, third, that they were taken completely by surprise as they had no reason to believe from intelligence sources that invasion was imminent.'

On Monday 26 June, Kim Il-sung again took to the air:

'Dear brothers and sisters! Great danger threatens our motherland and its people. What is needed to liquidate this menace? In this war which is being waged against the Syngman Rhee clique, the Korean people must defend the Korean Democratic People's Republic and its constitution, they must liquidate the unpatriotic fascist puppet regime of Syngman Rhee which has been established in the southern part of the republic; they must liberate the southern part of our motherland from the domination of the Syngman Rhee clique; and they must restore the people's committees there – the real organs of power. Under the banner of the Korean Democratic People's Republic we must complete the unification of the motherland and create a single, independent, democratic state. The war which we are forced to wage is a just war for the unification and independence of the motherland and for freedom and democracy...'

Just a few hours later the rumble of tanks could be heard, as they rolled into Seoul, the capital of the Republic of Korea.

The Summer of Terror

Two days after the invasion by North Korea, President Rhee came down hard on communists and communist sympathisers. He had forced about 300,000 people who were communists or were suspected of being communists to enrol in a re-education movement known as the Bodo League (also known as the National Rehabilitation and Guidance League, the National Guard Alliance, the National Guidance Alliance, or Bodo Yeonmaeng). Rhee claimed that their enrolment would safeguard them against execution for their political beliefs. However, in order to bolster numbers, non-communists were also forced to enrol in the league.

On 27 June 1950, Rhee issued an order that people associated with either the Bodo League or affiliated to the South Korean Workers' Party were to be executed. A day later, in Hoengseong in Ganwon-do, prisoners alleged to be communists and many members of the Bodo League were summarily executed by retreating South Korean troops and anti-communist groups. The chief of the Seoul Metropolitan Police later admitted to personally killing 12 people who were either communists or suspected of being communists after the start of the war. Following the recapture of Seoul in September 1950, around 30,000 South Koreans were executed by South Korean forces on suspicion of having collaborated while the North Koreans occupied the city.

Official United States documents demonstrate that US Army officers witnessed and photographed the massacre and it is known that one officer sanctioned the execution of political prisoners in order to prevent them falling into the hands of the enemy. Another document, however, shows the United States Ambassador to South Korea, John Muccio, recommending to the South Korean president and his defence minister, Shin Sung-mo (1891-1960), that the executions be stopped. When General MacArthur was informed of the massacre, he brushed it off as an 'internal matter'.

The actions of the South Korean troops were brutal. One witness describes 40 people having their backs broken with rifle butts and then being shot. In villages on the coast, victims were tied together and thrown into the sea to drown. One South Korean admiral admitted to having ordered around 200 people to be disposed of in this way, claiming that, 'there was no time for trials for them'. When the British, who had made strenuous efforts to stop their allies being murdered and, indeed, saved many people, raised the issue of atrocities, Dean Rusk (1909-94) informed them that senior US officers were doing everything they could to prevent the murders. Estimates of how many actually died during this period vary, but experts on the war reckon that between 60,000 and 110,000 were slaughtered. For many years, the murders were said to have been committed by the communists. Survivors concealed the truth on pain of torture or death but corpses began to be excavated from mass graves in the 1990s, bringing the massacre to the attention of the public.

A Fat Nation

It came as a complete surprise to the United States Government when North Korea invaded the south. In US defence policy at the end of the Second World War, Korea had been deemed to be of little importance and, given the straitened financial times, some even advocated the withdrawal of troops from the peninsula. Meanwhile, relations between the North and the South deteriorated badly during 1949, with many incidents on the 38th Parallel, perpetrated by both sides, leading to an atmosphere of complete mutual mistrust. The Americans remained convinced that, with US military training and with 'advisers' in place, ROK troops could deal with any aggression from the North.

By March 1950, however, a more pragmatic view was taken by Brigadier General WL Roberts, commander of the American Military Assistance Group in Korea. In a letter to the Pentagon, he warned:

'All G-2 sources tell that the North Koreans have up to 100 Russian planes and a training program for pilots. You know and I know what 100 planes can do to troops, to towns and to transport on roads. So, if South Korea were attacked today by the inferior [sic] ground forces of North Korea plus their Air Corps, I feel that South Korea would take a bloody nose. Again then, knowing these people somewhat, I feel they would follow the apparent winner and South Korea would be gobbled up to be added to the rest of Red Asia. This is a fat nation now with all its ECA goods, with warehouses bulging with plenty of rice from a good crop even if their finances are shaky with great inflationary tendencies. It is getting into the position of an excellent prize of war; strategically it points right into the heart of Japan and in the hands of an enemy it weakens the Japanese bastion of Western defense.'

The Russians had withdrawn their forces from North Korea by December 1948 and the Americans were reluctant to commit their forces to Asia. In fact, by the summer of 1950, Americans were more concerned about the loss of China to the communists than the threat of North Korea. The US had invested heavily in Chiang Kai-shek's nationalist forces during the war – $645 million in aid and more than $800 million in Lend-Lease – and around $2 billion had been handed over since the end of the Second World War. The fall of China led many Americans to believe that they should not be supporting anti-communist regimes such as Syngman Rhee's. Thus, American troops had been withdrawn by 29 June 1949.

This left a South Korean army of eight divisions – around 98,000 men, only 65,000 of whom had received adequate training. They also lacked planes, heavy artillery and tanks. Meanwhile, the North Korean People's Army was being revamped in the early months of 1950. In February 1948, elements of the Korean Volunteer Corps, which had been formed in Yan'an in China in 1939 and which had fought with the Chinese communist forces against the Japanese, were merged with resistance groups from the Soviet zone to form a formidable force. There was something of a power struggle, however, between those who wanted to adhere to Maoist tactical doctrine, which used the guerrilla strategy that defeated Chiang Kai-shek, and those who followed the traditional Soviet Red Army strategy of using armour and artillery. The Soviet faction won out.

By June 1950, the NKPA had seven divisions that were combat-ready. There were also three other newly constituted divisions as well as two independent regiments and an armoured brigade that was increased to division size – roughly 10–15,000 men – shortly after the outbreak of war. The army was well-trained and well-equipped and in addition to being well-supplied with artillery, it also had the formidable Soviet T-34 tank. Five brigades of the paramilitary Border Constabulary took the numerical strength of the NKPA to around 135,000 men. In terms of aircraft, the Korean People's Armed Forces Air Corps consisted of 150 to 200 planes, mostly Russian Yak-9 fighters and Ilyushin-10 ground attack bombers.

Washington and General MacArthur believed that there might be a certain amount of guerrilla activity and psychological warfare, but were adamant that there was little likelihood of a North Korean invasion in the summer of 1950. With this in mind, the US defence perimeter in the Pacific did not include Korea and even Formosa (later Taiwan), like Korea, was left to its own devices or the support of the United Nations in the event of trouble. Some intelligence reports, however, suggested that the North Koreans were preparing to invade, one even setting the date – June 1950. It is likely that such reports were lost in the plethora of communist threats coming in from around the world.

It remains unclear as to exactly why Kim Il-sung decided to invade the Republic of Korea in June 1950 but the attack would certainly have been sanctioned by the Soviets. Kim would not have been able to launch it without arms and supplies provided by Moscow and the help of the Chinese in allowing these to be transported across Chinese territory by rail. He travelled to Moscow to discuss his plans for war with the Soviet leader, Stalin. Kim convinced him that victory would be swift, and received his blessing, although Stalin confirmed that Russia would not become involved directly. Meanwhile, the Chinese leader, Mao Zedong, concurred with the view that the United States would stay out of any conflict on the Korean peninsula.

The invasion began with an artillery and mortar barrage at 4am on 25 June, which in Washington was the early afternoon of Saturday 24 June. Facing the NKPA was a Republic of Korea army with no armour or anti-tank weapons and no artillery heavier than 105mm. To make matters worse, the army had a reserve of only six days' ammunition while more than a third of the ROK's army vehicles were in need of repair, and there were no spare parts with which to make those repairs. Only about a third of Rhee's army was actually deployed on the line that faced the overwhelming North Korean assault.

Across the 38th Parallel

The communists drove south, through gaps in the hills, the impervious armour of their tanks rendering ROK resistance futile. In all, ten divisions, supported by 1,643 guns, crossed the 38th Parallel. The city of Kaesong, in the west, was the target for the NKPA 1st Division, while the 3rd and 4th Divisions captured the Uijongbu corridor. In the east, where the 5th Division attacked, the ROK front rapidly fell apart. ROK troops turned and began to flee southwards, often abandoning their weapons and equipment as they went.

At 9.30, Kim Il-sung took to the airwaves to provide the North Korean version of the morning's events:

'The South Korean puppet clique has rejected all methods for peaceful reunification proposed by the Democratic People's Republic of Korea, and dared to commit armed aggression... north of the 38th parallel... The Democratic People's Republic of Korea ordered a counter-attack to repel the invading troops. The South Korean puppet clique will be held responsible for whatever results may be brought about by this development.'

It was rapidly becoming clear to the American ambassador to South Korea that this was more than just another skirmish, as he was at pains to point out in a cable to his superiors in Washington:

'North Korean forces invaded Republic of Korea at several places this morning... It would appear from the nature of the attack and the manner in which it was launched that it constitutes an all-out offensive against the Republic of Korea.'

The United Nations was based temporarily that summer at Lake Success, New York, where, on the afternoon of 25 June, the Security Council was hurriedly assembled. One notable absentee was Yakov Malik (1906-80), the Soviet Union delegate. He had walked out on 13 January in protest at the organisation's refusal to replace Nationalist China with the People's Republic of China and, with the nationalists still in situ, the USSR had not returned to the Security Council. Nonetheless, a resolution was unanimously passed that condemned the North Korean invasion and demanded the withdrawal of all North Korean troops south of the 38th Parallel. It would be the only time in UN history that such a stance was taken and, of course, it was made possible only by the Soviet Union's empty chair.

It should be noted how febrile the atmosphere was at that time. Communism's spread was perceived to be a huge problem by the West. It was gaining ground in Europe, where the nations of the east of the continent had moved into the Soviet sphere and it was feared that Greece, France and Italy were also in danger of turning communist. In the Middle East, Asia and Latin America, the doctrine was also making inroads. Thus, when Kim Il-sung invaded the Republic of Korea without much of a pretext for doing so, there was horror around the globe. Some believed the invasion to be a huge miscalculation by Kim, and that Syngman Rhee's regime was so corrupt and inept that it would have collapsed eventually anyway. But suddenly, Rhee found himself occupying the moral high ground whilst also enjoying the support of the United Nations.

The United States was placed in an invidious position. As Secretary of State Dean Acheson (1893-1971) later wrote:

'Plainly this attack did not amount to a *casus belli* against the Soviet Union. Equally plainly, it was an open, undisguised challenge to our internationally accepted position as the protector of South Korea, an area of great importance to the security of American-occupied

Japan. To back away from this challenge, in view of our capacity for meeting it, would be highly destructive of the power and prestige of the United States.'

But did America have the 'capacity for meeting [the threat]'? It is to be doubted because, as has been noted previously, at that point there was a lack of enthusiasm for involvement in Korea and US forces were being withdrawn from the peninsula. Some Republicans opposed financial aid to South Korea and the country did not seem to figure in US plans for the region. Furthermore, the armed forces of the USA had been reduced from 12 million troops at the end of the war to just 1.6 million. Spending had fallen commensurately, from $82 to $13 billion, leading to shortfalls in training and equipment. Still, Truman's administration was keen to resist the challenge presented by North Korea's aggression, especially as it was unquestionably being supported and encouraged by the Soviet Union in an effort to diminish American and Western influence in the Far East.

The day of the invasion, President Truman decided to order General MacArthur to withdraw the 2,000 American service personnel in South Korea and he ordered MacArthur to provide South Korea with as much equipment and ammunition as possible from Japan. He also extended MacArthur's area of command to include Formosa. To discourage the Chinese or Chiang Kai-shek's nationalists from increasing tensions in the Far

East, the US Seventh Fleet was positioned between Formosa and China, an action described by Chinese premier Zhou Enlai as 'armed aggression on Chinese territory'. On the American side, however, there was a concern that the invasion was perhaps just the first step in communist actions around the world.

'Things are not going well militarily'

On 26 June, Syngman Rhee contacted his diplomats in Washington and asked them to plead with President Truman for help and especially for arms. At first, they were disappointed with the president's lukewarm response to their pleas but the following day they learned that Truman had shifted his position and was now promising air and naval support. It was a controversial decision, as General MacArthur suggested:

'I could not help being amazed at the manner in which this great decision was being made. With no submission to Congress, whose duty it is to declare war, and without even consulting the field commander involved, the members of the executive branch... agreed to enter the Korean War... All the risks inherent in this decision – including the possibility of Chinese and Russian involvement – applied then just as much as they applied later.'

On 27 June, three days after the invasion, the United Nations passed a resolution that called upon its member nations to 'render such assistance to the Republic of Korea as may be necessary to repel the armed attack and to restore international peace and security to the area'. Yugoslavia, as might have been expected, abstained and the vote was carried by seven to one. It was becoming evident that Truman was now prepared to stop the communists in Korea at any cost. It was, after all, an opportunity for the administration – often described by its Republican opponents as being weak on communism – to demonstrate its willingness to be tough on the communist threat.

The State Department contacted American allies, countries such as Britain, Australia and France, and asked whether they would consider providing forces to be used to implement the UN resolution with General MacArthur as commander of those forces. It would be a demanding job and there were many who questioned the wisdom of appointing a 70-year-old to the position. There were also questions as to whether he had the skills appropriate to the role. The commander of these troops would have to be not just a soldier but also a diplomat and a statesman and, as James Reston wrote of MacArthur in *The New York Times*:

'[He] is a sovereign power in his own right, with stubborn confidence in his own judgement. Diplomacy and a vast concern for the opinions and sensitivities of others are the political qualities essential to this new assignment, and these are precisely the qualities General MacArthur has been accused of lacking in the past.'

Nonetheless, Truman's decision to make a stand against communism in Korea proved popular with the American people. It was viewed as courageous, a sign that America was taking its great post-war responsibilities seriously. Congress liked it too, and just an hour after the President's announcement, a bill was passed, by 314 votes to 4, extending the draft. A few days later, the Military Assistance Programme for Korea passed unanimously in the Senate.

For MacArthur, confrontation with the forces of communism had always seemed inevitable. But he was also concerned that the Russians would soon catch up with the United States in the nuclear arms race and that the advantage his country enjoyed would be lost. Thus, he reasoned, it was better to take on the communists before it got to that point.

MacArthur had firm views on the nature of warfare and the notion of limited warfare was anathema to him. He believed in engaging in all-out war until the enemy was defeated. He also had the deeply-held belief that a general on a field of battle should be the one making the decisions. It had worked for him during the Second World War in the Pacific and he fully expected to be given free rein once more to wage war as he saw fit.

General Douglas MacArthur

Douglas MacArthur was born into a military family in Little Rock Barracks, Little Rock, Arkansas and his father would eventually rise to the rank of Lieutenant General in the army. MacArthur attended West Texas Military Academy and West Point where he was First Captain – the most senior cadet – and graduated top of his class in 1903. In 1914, he was nominated for the Medal of Honor, America's highest personal military decoration, for leading a reconnaissance mission during the United States occupation of Veracruz in Mexico. When America entered the First World War, MacArthur fought on the Western Front, holding the rank of Major, but he was soon promoted to colonel. He became chief of staff of the 42nd (Rainbow) Division of the United States Army National Guard. By the time of the armistice, he had been promoted to Brigadier General, had once again been nominated for the Medal of Honor, had twice been awarded the Distinguished Service Cross and had won the Silver Star no fewer than seven times.

Back in the United States, from 1919 until 1922 MacArthur served as superintendent of West Point before he was sent to the Philippines in 1924 where he helped to quell a mutiny by the Philippine Scouts, an auxiliary unit to the US Army. He was promoted to Major General the following year, the youngest man ever to hold that rank. In 1930, he was appointed chief of staff of the Army but he retired from the Army seven years later to become a military adviser to the Commonwealth Government of the Philippines.

When America entered the Second World War in 1941, MacArthur returned to active duty as commander of the United States Army Forces in the Far East. It did not begin well. His air power was eliminated by the Japanese on 8 December 1941, the day after their attack on Pearl Harbor. On the same day, they invaded the Philippines, forcing the US Asiatic fleet to withdraw to Bataan four days later. MacArthur was ordered out of the area in March 1942 and travelled to Australia, leaving his 76,000 starving and sick American and Filipino troops to surrender the following month. When MacArthur reached Australia, he famously promised 'I shall return' to the Philippines. Interestingly, Washington requested that he change 'I shall return' to 'we shall return'. Naturally, he ignored the request.

Appointed Supreme Commander, Southwest Pacific Area, MacArthur fulfilled his promise two years later, receiving the Medal of Honor for his defence of the Philippines. On 2 September 1945, he accepted the surrender of the Japanese on board USS *Missouri* in Tokyo Bay and he remained in Japan until 1951, supervising the Allied occupation. In 1951, war in Korea brought him, at the age of 70, another opportunity to burnish his reputation as one of America's greatest generals.

To some, it seemed as if MacArthur believed himself to be above the normal rules of everyday existence. He should have been held to account for the military disaster that unfolded in the Philippines between 1941 and 1942, but he came out of it squeaky clean. He could have been criticised for abandoning his men on Bataan. After he left, complete with family and staff – often described as sycophantic and derisively known as 'the Bataan gang' – his troops endured the dreadful 100-kilometre Bataan Death March at the hands of the Japanese. There are differing casualty numbers but somewhere between 5,650 and 18,000 Filipinos are reported to have died during the march and 500 to 650 Americans. Many questioned his flight, but it has been pointed out that he was too valuable to be left to be captured with his men. There has also been a great deal of controversy about a large financial gift to him from the president of the Philippines, Manuel Quezon (1878-1944).

However, he still commanded respect, firstly from the American people for victory over Japan in the war and secondly from the Japanese themselves, for pardoning the country for its actions in the war. He had even made a stab at the US presidency in 1948, but had failed to gain the Republican nomination. Remarkably, he did not set foot in the United States between 1936 and 1948.

3

The West Responds

MacArthur Visits Korea and Comes up with a Plan

On 28 June, the North Koreans took Seoul. The following day, American planes began to arrive in Suwon in the north-west of the country, carrying ammunition and supplies from Japan. MacArthur himself arrived, together with a party of journalists. There had been a scary moment while the plane was in the air when an enemy fighter approached, only to be chased away by the American Mustangs accompanying the general's aircraft. While everyone on board was terrified, MacArthur is reported to have watched the encounter with fascination, not at all perturbed by it. He was met at Suwon by Ambassador John J Muccio (1900-89), a visibly shaken Syngman Rhee and Brigadier John Church (1892-1953) who briefed the visitors. MacArthur spent about eight hours travelling around the battlefield, inspecting the damage and, most importantly, of course, being photographed as he did so.

The capital was, by this time, already in North Korean hands. MacArthur later reported that, as he looked upon the refugees flocking south, South Korean soldiers amongst them, and gazed at the columns of smoke from artillery bombardments on the horizon, he came up with the notion of a great amphibious landing that would launch the fightback. On his return to Tokyo, he dispatched a report to Washington, complete with his recommendation that the North Koreans could only be defeated by the entry into the situation of US ground forces. Admittedly, he acknowledged, his Occupation Army was far from battle-ready, but time was of the essence and there was not enough of it to train or re-equip. 'Unless provision is made,' he wrote, 'for the full utilization of the Army-Navy-Air team in this shattered area, our mission will at best be needlessly costly in life, money and prestige. At worst, it might even be doomed to failure.' It was evident from his report that he was thinking about more than just pushing the NKPA out of South Korea; he was intent on the destruction of North Korea.

Truman was at his desk early on the morning of 29 June. He discussed with Dean Acheson the offer of Nationalist China leader Chiang Kai-shek of 33,000 of his troops to be sent to Korea to join the UN force. Acheson very quickly pointed out that the involvement of the Chinese nationalists would inevitably bring Mao's China into play on the peninsula. For their part, the Joint Chiefs of Staff were dubious about the quality of troops that Chiang could make available and the idea was vetoed. Initially, therefore, it was going to be Americans who would confront the NKPA and they would be drawn from the Occupying Army in Japan.

Orders were dispatched to MacArthur's headquarters in Tokyo and, shortly after that, the proposed actions were divulged to the world. There would be a naval blockade of the whole Korean coast; the United States Air Force in the Far East was to be mobilised into action against the North Koreans; and ground units would be flown to Korea. The troops of the 24th Division suddenly found themselves having to adapt from the quiet life of an occupying force to a unit going to war. It was not a promising prospect but, if America had done nothing at that point, South Korea would undoubtedly have fallen to the communists. There was a belief, too, that no matter how ill-prepared, American troops would still be more than enough for Kim Il-sung's army.

Meanwhile, the question was how many United Nations member states would step up to help?

The Allies Rally

Although a victor in the Second World War, Britain, like the rest of Europe, was suffering economically. Food rationing, shortages and economic and industrial difficulties persisted well into the 1950s. Clement Attlee's Labour Party had won a surprising landslide victory over Winston Churchill's Conservatives in 1945 and it was re-elected in 1950 with a slim majority. The war had cost Britain some £7,000 million and against an annual rate of imports of £1,100 million, it raised only £400 million annually in exports. The country survived on American loans and, indeed, the welfare state, a crowning achievement of Attlee's Labour government, came into being only through American borrowings. As well as the loans, there was also money from the Marshall Plan, or European Recovery Plan, a gift of $12 billion, to be divided amongst the recovering nations of Europe. Of this, Britain received the largest amount, about 26 per cent of the total sum. But relations between the two countries were not great. Many MPs on the government side were deeply anti-American, while the United States was less than impressed by Britain's handling of its mandate in Palestine.

At the end of the war, Britain was spending around a fifth of her Gross National Product on defence and, indeed, there were still 1.5 million men and women in the services. Defence spending was still huge in 1951, and large tracts of the world continued to be under British control. Even more money went on the development of Britain's atomic bomb. Despite the suspicion of America, however, the Cold War brought the two nations together and made Moscow the enemy, especially after the 1949 Soviet blockade of Berlin, the communists' attempt to gain control in Greece and the threat the Soviet Union was posing to British interests in the Middle East.

On 27 June, the British cabinet met and Korea was on the agenda. It emerged that ministers were reluctant to accept that the North Korean invasion was driven by Moscow in an attempt to further the cause of communism. It was suggested that if the notion of a communist conspiracy, directed by Moscow, was promulgated, the Soviet Union would be antagonised and would be rendered unable to withdraw support from North Korea without losing face. The British also feared for their relationship with China and its impact on the status of the British colony of Hong Kong. The Americans had a deep distrust of communist China, but the British accepted its existence as a fact of life and one with which they had to live.

Nonetheless, Britain was resolved to provide support for the United States and the United Nations in the battle to thwart North Korean plans in the peninsula. She acted immediately, much to the relief of the Truman administration. The Royal Navy's Far East fleet was dispatched to the seas around Korea to support the US Navy, an action widely supported in Britain. One facet of the American approach did not sit well with the British Chiefs of Staff, however. It was suggested that should the UN/US efforts not be successful, the next step would be for America to use the atom bomb in Korea. The Chiefs of Staff decided that this would be 'unsound'. 'The effects of such action would be worldwide, and might well be very damaging. Moreover, it would probably provoke a global war.'

These senior British military personages were also unhappy about the prospects of Britain being asked to commit ground troops, citing military reasons for their antipathy. They were in no doubt, like the Americans, that Moscow was behind the North Korean invasion, but they were of the opinion that the action in Korea was no more than a diversionary tactic; that there would be another incident, possibly even in Europe. Furthermore, there had been very little money since the war to lavish on equipment and the British army was seriously understrength in many areas around the world where a British military presence had to be maintained.

In a debate on the matter on 5 July, Prime Minister Attlee said: 'I think that no one can have any doubt whatever that here is a case of naked aggression. Surely, with the history of the last twenty years fresh in our minds, no one can doubt that it is vitally important that aggression should be halted at the outset.' The leader of the opposition, the former prime minister, Winston Churchill, agreed and congratulated Attlee on his approach, offering his party's full support. The Conservative MP for Taunton, Henry Hopkinson, summed up the excitement that was felt in the chamber of the House of Commons that day:

'I should like to remark that we are, in fact, witnessing something quite unique in the enforcement by arms of collective security by a world organization… That is something that has never before occurred in the history of the world and it is, at least, a consolation that we are moving along the lines towards an international police force.'

Task Force Smith and the Battle of Osan

Task Force Smith consisted of 406 men of the 1st Battalion, 21st Infantry Regiment, and 134 men of A Battery, 52nd Field Artillery Battalion. Some of them had seen action in World War II – about a third of the officers and a sixth of the soldiers – but the unit consisted mostly of teenagers, who had done little more than their eight weeks of basic training and had zero combat experience. Badly understrength and poorly equipped, they had been softened by years of comfortable occupation duty in Japan. Nonetheless, the 21st Infantry had been selected by Division Commander, Major General William F Dean (1899-1981), because he believed it was the most combat-ready of the three regiments of the 24th Division. They may not have had much battlefield experience but their commander, Lieutenant Colonel Charles Bradford 'Brad' Smith (1916-2004), was the most experienced commanding officer in the Division, having fought at Guadalcanal. Smith's orders from Dean were nothing if not succinct:

'When you go to Pusan, head for Taejon. We want to stop the North Koreans as far from Pusan as we can. Block the main road as far north as possible. Make contact with General Church. If you can't find him, go to Taejon and beyond if you can. Sorry I can't give you more information – that's all I've got. Good luck, and God bless you and your men!'

On 30 June 1950, five days after the North Korean People's Army had launched their invasion, the American troops were airlifted from Itazuke Air Base, on the island of Kyushu in the south of Japan, and flown to Pusan in the south of the ROK. The NKPA was now making progress south rapidly, virtually unopposed by the South Korean army. Task Force Smith began its advance north, transported by rail and road, passing long, snaking lines of refugees fleeing the invaders and sleeping where they could. Mosquitoes were a scourge, the water made people sick and the smell of human faeces filled the air; the Koreans used it to fertilise their paddy fields.

On the night of 4 July, the American troops were ordered to block the Suwon Road about 50 miles south of Seoul, the country's capital, which had, by this time, fallen to the communists. Reportedly, one US Army colonel remarked to Lieutenant Colonel Smith that the task force resembled 'a bunch of boy scouts'. As they moved forward on hilly ground, three miles north of the small town of Osan, they had been told they would meet South Korean troops, but, encountering none, they started digging in, rain and difficult terrain hampering their efforts. A thousand yards behind them 105mm howitzers were located.

The first sight of the enemy came shortly after 7am the following day, when a column of eight green tanks – formidable Russian-built T-34s – trundled along the open plain from the direction of the town of Suwon. The howitzer operators were given the coordinates and opened fire, but, unfortunately, their shells lacked armour-piercing capability, and were inadequate for the task. A 75mm recoilless rifle similarly failed to make an impression on the advancing tanks, as did a bazooka. What they required was the more lethal 3.5-inch rocket launcher but a decision had been made not to issue that particular weapon to the US Army of the Far East. In fact, the bazooka was fired no fewer than 22 times, but made no impression on the tanks' relentless advance. Only one was intercepted, one of its tracks having broken, but it continued to fire on the Americans with both its large main gun and its machine gun. As another armoured platoon approached, the only 105mm gun the Americans possessed managed to stop one tank which burst into flames. An American soldier – Kenneth Shadrick (1931-50) – was gunned down by the T-34's machine gun. He is often given the unenviable distinction of being the first American soldier to die in the Korean War, although subsequent investigations have cast doubt on this.

Around 30 T-34's rolled past the 'blocking position' occupied by the troops of Task Force Smith before

9.30am and, about 90 minutes later, three more tanks appeared at the head of a column of trucks. Stopping up the road, before they reached the task force's position, they disgorged thousands of NKPA troops, many of whom disappeared into the paddy fields that lined the road. Others advanced directly on the American positions, while some spread out to the east and west flanks. American casualties began to mount and Smith and his officers decided to form a circular perimeter on their eastern flank. There was little else they could do. To withdraw and head south would merely bring his men into contact with the tanks that had earlier passed through their position. And launching a counter-attack against the communists was unlikely to succeed, especially as the prospect of reinforcements being brought in was remote. As ammunition began to run out, the NKPA mortars were taking their toll.

Facing an impossible dilemma, Smith took the only decision he could; he decided to withdraw. Of course, escape along the road was out of the question, as the Americans would be easy meat for the enemy machine guns. Therefore, his troops were forced to drop down into the flooded paddy fields, and before long it was every man for himself as they scrabbled away from the battle, throwing away their weapons and equipment.

The men of the 21st walked in groups for up to a week, often carrying their wounded, but leaving behind those who were too badly injured, to be taken prisoner. Eventually, 185 men made it to American positions. The task force had suffered 155 casualties in the engagement at Osan. Their failings as a unit were overshadowed, however, by other American setbacks as the NKPA swept all before it as it proceeded down the length of the Korean peninsula.

The catastrophic defeat of Task Force Smith would not be the last humiliation the United States military would face during the long and painful three years of the Korean War.

The Pusan Perimeter

To begin with, the North Korean army had an air of invincibility about it. Kim Il-sung had set 15 August, the fifth anniversary of VJ Day, as the date by which all of Korea would be in his hands and his army seemed to be well on their way to achieving this. By the end of June, just under a week into the invasion, more than half of the ROK army had been wiped out. Defence economies were badly affecting the Eighth Army in Japan, reduced to 70 per cent of its full strength. MacArthur had just 92 tanks under his command and they were proving too heavy for Korean roads.

South of Seoul, the North Koreans had stopped in order to reorganise themselves and to ensure they did not get too far ahead of their means of resupply. Moving again on 5 July, they immediately came into contact with Task Force Smith behind which the rest of the US

24th Division was being deployed. Headed by Major General William Dean, it established its HQ in Taejon while, around it, the South Korean army appeared to be in chaos and engaged in a retreat. The US Air Force was dropping huge quantities of bombs on Korea but it did not really make much of an impact upon the advancing invaders.

The 1,981 soldiers of the 34th Infantry, moving into place behind Task Force Smith, were next to come into contact with the enemy after Smith's men were routed. They were poorly equipped, with no tanks or decent anti-tank weapons and, because they had been hastily transported from Japan, they were not well prepared for battle. Dean ordered them to block key roads south at Ansong and Pyongtaek. Later on that 5 July night, however, the remnants of Task Force Smith began to arrive at their positions, after being overwhelmed by the North Koreans. Soon the enemy appeared with T-34 tanks and, after engaging them with mortars and machine guns, the commander of the 1/34th ordered his men to retreat to prevent them being cut off. Throwing away weapons and equipment, the Americans fled ingloriously amongst a long line of fleeing refugees. Dean was furious when he learned what was happening and ordered them to dig in where they were and fight.

Unfortunately, in those first few weeks of the war, this became the pattern. The refugees would stream towards American positions, and then their long train would suddenly dry up and the tanks would appear, trundling towards them. Infantrymen would next arrive, swarming around the tanks and overwhelming the Americans who would be forced to retreat. It was one of the worst-ever periods for the US Army and the blame for the failure to provide an effective defence had to fall squarely on the shoulders of the officers and the tactics they employed. There were ways they could have interrupted and stalled the apparently irresistible advance of the enemy. For instance, they could have struck the NKPA, held them with mortar and machine-gun fire and then withdrawn to another position, thus wearing the enemy down. Anti-tank obstacles, to deter the movement of the T-34s, could have been deployed but, for some unknown reason, never were. Mines, when they eventually became available, were never used and neither were the support weapons they had.

MacArthur was appointed Commander-in-Chief of the United Nations force on 10 July. The Americans had insisted on direct control being given to him, instead of being placed in the hands of the Committee on Coordination for the Assistance of Korea, as Britain, France and Norway had wanted. Ultimately, the war was largely conducted under the auspices of American politicians and military men. On 13 July, General Walton Walker (1889-1950), who had been a corps commander in Europe under the controversial General George S Patton (1885-1945), established the headquarters for his Eighth Army in Korea. He was given operational responsibility for the UN ground forces and ordered by

MacArthur not to give an inch. Unfortunately, his troops were brushed aside by the North Koreans who deployed along the Geum River. Encircled, the 19th Infantry was compelled to fight its way out, with heavy casualties, and was forced back to Taejon. The North Koreans fought their way into the city and the soldiers of the 24th were once again retreating southwards, losing about 30 per cent of their colleagues. After wandering in the hills, a fugitive for months after Taejon fell, the commander of the 24th, Major General Dean, was captured, becoming the most senior American officer taken prisoner by the communists in the entire war. He would be welcomed home as a hero at the end of the conflict.

Troops continued to arrive. The US 25th Division landed between 10 and 15 July and, on 18 July, the infantrymen of the 1st Cavalry made shore at Pohang on Korea's south-eastern coast, but, in the meantime, Americans were retreating and fleeing on all fronts, abandoning weapons and equipment as they did so. Suicidal North Korean troops threw themselves at the American lines, a practice that only got worse as the conflict progressed. The Koreans ignored the rules of war, using soldiers dressed in civilian clothes, pretending to surrender and then attacking, and they were ruthless in the manner in which they dealt with captives. There was widespread revulsion in America when groups of US troops were discovered shot at the roadside, hands grotesquely tied behind their backs with barbed wire. Of course, this also had the effect of focusing the minds of the Americans; better to fight than to be taken prisoner and treated abominably.

What was termed the 'bug-out' – flight from the battlefield – was still very common, especially when troops were afraid of being outflanked and cut off. They often found themselves in isolated positions, perhaps separated by 20 or 30 miles of mountainous terrain from the nearest Allied troops. Fears of bad treatment led Americans to lump all Koreans – 'gooks', as they were called by the soldiers – together. They were bewildered by their language, their customs and their attitude to life and death. This resulted in a callousness on the part of the Americans towards them all, whether they originated from the North or the South.

But heavy losses were sustained by the North Koreans – some 58,000 casualties between the start of the war and August. The Allied forces, in fact, now outnumbered the North Koreans but, despite this, Allied troops were at a low ebb. The 25th Division held its line in the centre of South Korea but was forced to withdraw on 30 July; the 1st Cavalry had started its retreat in the direction of Kumchong the previous day. Meanwhile, a North Korean division was pushing southward, pretty much unopposed, in the west of the country and, by 1 August, the forward units of that division had reached as far as Masan which lay just 30 miles from the south-eastern port of Pusan. If they made it to Pusan, the Americans would find themselves encircled by the enemy. The situation was so desperate that Walker dispatched men of the 25th Division there to try to bring the advance to a halt. The Americans formed a new defensive line, taking up the high ground behind the Naktong River. It would be either the last stand of the UN force or the start of a new phase of the war. As Walker told his men:

'There will be no more retreating, withdrawal, readjustment of lines or whatever you call it. There are no lines behind which we can retreat. This is not going to be a Dunkirk or Bataan. A retreat to Pusan would result in one of the greatest butcheries in history. We must fight to the end. We must fight as a team. If some of us die, we will die fighting together.'

The Naktong River was shallow enough in places to be easily fordable but, to the advantage of the Americans, it had steep hills on each bank. The river made up half of the UN defensive line. With good observation points, fighter attacks on enemy positions were particularly effective. Nonetheless, Walker's men were low in spirits and morale, and their training had been inadequate for what was being asked of them. To make matters worse, Walker did not have enough troops to patrol the entire 130-mile line properly. Reinforcements were arriving, however, in the form of the British Marines of 27 Brigade and there were 45,000 South Korean soldiers who could be called upon, although most of them were untrained and had actually been forced from their villages into the army at gunpoint.

As has been noted, the UN force now outnumbered the North Koreans and was certainly better equipped than them. The North Koreans' supplies were beginning to run out and the suicidal nature of many of their attacks was reducing their strength even further. Nonetheless, on the night of 5 August, the NKPA forded the Naktong, overwhelming the American forward positions. For the next few days, they built up their strength on the east bank of the river and began to push forward. But, on 17 August, a US counter-attack forced them back across the river. Meanwhile, to the north, the Eighth Army HQ at Taegu came under threat and, by 15 August, three North Korean divisions were 15 miles from the town, ready to launch an attack. A couple of other divisions, trying to link up with them, were pushed back by the Americans while the US Air Force pounded North Korean positions day and night. Ultimately, although, because it was summer, the Naktong was at its lowest level and easily fordable, the North Koreans failed to take advantage, unable to reinforce and resupply. They withdrew and Walker could begin to focus on Taegu.

The Battle of the Bowling Alley was the name given to the week-long clash north of Taegu. It was so named because of the steep-sided valley in which it was contested. The 25th Division's task was to prevent the North Koreans from breaking through and, by 24 August, they had succeeded. Meanwhile, the ROK 3rd Division was forced back in the north- eastern section of the perimeter and Pohang was lost to the NKPA but retaken a few days later after American reinforcements arrived to support the South Korean troops. It became evident that the communist effort in the area was beginning to flag.

The last days of August saw the communists regrouping and there was something of a pause in the fighting on the Pusan Perimeter. They devised a new strategy, realising that attacking at different points on the line had been a mistake. Now they prepared a coordinated assault, their 6th and 7th Divisions attacking the US 25th Division in the south at Masan while the 2nd, 4th, 9th and 10th readied themselves for an attack on what was known as the Naktong Bulge, defended by the US 2nd Division. To the north, Taegu would also be hit. The North Koreans struck on the last night of August, breaking through the line held by the US 25th and placing Masan in danger. North of there, they overran the 2nd Division around Taegu. Waegwan was lost, forcing Walker to move his HQ to Pusan. Pohang was lost once again and it looked as if Walker would have to withdraw his men from right across the perimeter.

Suddenly, however, the advance withered and the Americans began to come out on top, helped by air and artillery support. The truth was that the NKPA was running out of both men and equipment. Walker had achieved what had seemed impossible; he had defended the Pusan Perimeter with an army that had no stomach for the fight and that lacked training as well as equipment. He ensured the survival of the United Nations force in Korea for the foreseeable future.

Meanwhile, in Britain...

Throughout the first three months of the conflict, the British Chiefs of Staff were dubious about the ability of the United Nations force to succeed in Korea. In fact, they believed that the UN army might even have to withdraw from the country and then reinvade at a later date and that it would take many months to assemble the troops and resources required for that future invasion. They favoured an air offensive to wipe out North Korea's industry and interrupt communications, but, while admitting that such an air offensive would not be guaranteed to bring Kim Il-sung to the negotiating table, they cautioned against the use of atomic weapons:

'...we shall be no worse off if it did not. We assume there will be no question of using the atomic bomb in Korea. This weapon must in our view be kept in reserve for use in the proper place in the event of a major war with Russia. Anyway, there are no suitable objectives for it in North Korea. This is a United Nations police action, and we do not want to kill thousands of civilians and create a radioactive shambles, but with the minimum loss of life and expense on either side, to restore the status quo and the integrity of South Korea.'

Naturally, Britain's hesitancy was irksome to Washington. As has already been noted, the Chiefs of

Staff, and others in America, were concerned that, while they flooded men and resources into Korea, the Soviets would attack somewhere else in the world. In such an event, the West would be powerless to stop them. They also feared the cost of this adventure, both in terms of resources and of men. But, on the other hand, they wholeheartedly embraced the idea of dealing with what was the current communist threat.

The British eventually decided that a division, at least, had to be sent and to do this meant recalling to uniform many reservists. Thus, the dreaded letters were sent out that summer, informing their recipients: 'In accordance with the terms of your reserve liability, it has become necessary to recall you to active military duty.' It was extremely upsetting for some, especially as the War Office made no distinction in who it called up. Even former prisoners of war were not exempt. Many were outraged, although there were those who, after the excitement of the war, were bored with life on civvy street and were eager to get back to action. Still more, however, had no real clue as to why they were being sent to fight in this faraway land. They quite simply felt that it was nothing whatsoever to do with them.

The troops were said by the War Office to be the best-equipped force ever to leave Britain, but it soon became clear that, in their equipment, transport and clothing, they lagged far behind the Americans. Not for nothing was the first contingent of British troops – the 1st Middlesex – nicknamed 'the Woolworth Brigade'. They had no specialist equipment for extremes of weather, no sleeping bags and just a few vehicles. Many were young conscripts who were bewildered by what they were being sent to do.

4

MacArthur's Miracle at Inchon

For and Against

MacArthur claimed to have first conceived of an amphibious landing at Inchon in the north-west of South Korea during his visit to Suwon on 29 June. Already aware that the North Koreans' supply lines would become very stretched during their advance southwards, he reasoned that he could add to this problem by staging a landing at Inchon and disrupting those supply lines, since Inchon to Seoul was the most important road and rail hub in Korea. He would also make life difficult for the enemy by opening a war on two fronts.

He had already carried out a daring assault, similar to the one he planned at Inchon, when, in February 1944, he had staged an amphibious landing on the Admiralty Islands. It had helped to shorten the war in the Pacific. He must also have been thinking about how his envelopment of Hollandia in New Guinea a couple of months later had outflanked an entire Japanese army. Inchon was an ideal place to attack. Seoul was just 18 miles to the east and to retake the capital would provide an enormous psychological boost to everyone on the UN side.

It was hard work obtaining permission for the operation, however. The plan was opposed by the Joint Chiefs of Staff, by naval officers in the Far East and by many other military men and specialists. Many of them, having carried out such operations during the Second World War, were all too aware of the many variables involved – tides, the gradient of the beach, fire support and the ability to unload the troops quickly. A number believed that the landing was actually planned for the wrong side of Korea but MacArthur, as ever, was adamant that he was right.

A landing at Inchon would be fraught with problems. Eleven hours before they effected the landing, the Americans would have to seize the offshore island of Wolmi-do, thus signalling to the North Koreans their presence in the area and the likelihood of an assault. Wolmi-do commanded the approaches to Inchon, making its capture essential. To make matters worse, typhoon season was approaching which meant the weather could be problematic and the surrounding hills could give the NKPA a vantage point from which to pour fire down on the American troops. Even the facility for handling cargo was fairly inadequate. The landing would have to be made in the evening, due to the tides, which would give them just two hours of daylight to secure a beachhead. It was going to be risky and even the Marines' commander, General Lemuel C Shepherd (1896-1990) was dubious about the possibility of success, viewing the communists as formidable enemies who would fight fanatically to defend Inchon.

MacArthur was obviously no fool and he also knew the risks involved. He was also fully aware that morale was low but he was nothing if not a man of the grand gesture and this was certainly just that. He was even going to commit forces from the defence of Pusan, so convinced was he that he would come out on top. At a meeting of MacArthur and all the commanders in the Far East, held at his headquarters in Tokyo, the Dai Ichi, he gave the performance of his life. He spoke for 45 minutes, urging and shaming the commanders, even implying that the mission's impossibility was exactly why they should attempt it:

'The very arguments you have made as to the impracticabilities involved will tend to ensure for me the element of surprise. For the enemy commander will reason that no one would be so brash as to make such an attempt... I can almost hear the ticking of the second hand of destiny. We must act now or we will die... We shall land at Inchon, and I shall crush them.'

Apparently, the Chief of Naval Operations reassured him that the Navy would get him to Inchon, but many left the meeting unconvinced. Finally, after other landing points had been rejected by him, MacArthur was given the go-ahead by the Joint Chiefs for a landing on 28 August.

The Landing at Inchon

Amidst a prevailing air of apprehension, MacArthur appointed his Chief of Staff, the fiercely ambitious Lieutenant General Edward Almond (1892-1979) as commander of the Inchon landing force. There would later be criticism of MacArthur for splitting the command in Korea between two men, Almond and Walker. He had, in fact, considered relieving Walker of his duties and giving Almond overall command, but knew that this would be unacceptable back home because 'Bulldog' Walker, as he was nicknamed, had been enjoying a high profile in the United States.

The pessimism of all the Americans but MacArthur was unwarranted. There seemed to be a view that the North Koreans had numerical superiority over the UN force, but the truth was that Kim Il-sung had only around 70,000 men while the United Nations troops under the command of General Walker numbered 140,000. Even better was the fact that the Allies enjoyed complete command of air and sea and possessed much greater firepower than the communists could muster. The communists' logistical and technical support was also very poor. Unfortunately, US security was also poor and the proposed landing at Inchon was common knowledge amongst the troops, although miraculously it seems never to have reached the ears of the military planners in Pyongyang. In the days before the boats sailed for Inchon, the North Koreans did nothing.

Agents who had been sent to Inchon to investigate the area, ascertained that there were just 500 North Korean troops on Wolmi-do and a mere 1,500 in the Inchon area, although, of course, reinforcements could quickly be drafted in. Therefore, to distract the North Koreans, British ships were detailed to unleash a bombardment on Chinnampo (now Nampo), a port in south-western North Korea and a raiding party was landed from a British frigate at Gunsan on the west coast of South Korea.

The Marine Corps designated to make the landing was commanded by the 57-year-old Texan, General Oliver Smith (1893-1977), a veteran of World War II, and an expert on amphibious warfare. MacArthur told him: 'I know that this operation will be a sort of helter-skelter. But the 1st Marine Division is going to win the war by landing at Inchon.' The landing was important not only for the future of the Korean War, but also for the future of the Marines. In the nuclear age, there was a growing conviction that they no longer had a role to play, that large-scale amphibious operations were a thing of the past. Smith recognised, therefore, that there was an opportunity to prove the value of his men, many of whom also had vast combat experience.

There would be 260 ships in all, the first of which left Yokohama on 5 September on the slow trip to Korea. Many of the vessels in which troops and equipment were transported were old. Some, that had seen service in World War II, had been transferred to the Japanese merchant navy but had now been recalled to duty with the Americans. MacArthur sailed from Sasebo on USS *Mount McKinley* on 13 September and the convoy reached the Inchon narrows shortly before dawn on 15 September. For the previous five days, the US Air Force had been bombarding Wolmi-do, in an effort to divert the attention of the communists from the real mission.

The first Marines landed on Wolmi-do at 6.33am and began their advance. By noon the first part of the operation was completed with very little resistance being shown by the communists. They now had to wait for the tide to turn while fighter planes patrolled the roads leading to Inchon ready to punish any attempts to bring forward reinforcements. Fortunately for the Americans, however, there was no sign of any back-up.

At 2.30pm, the ships once again began bombarding the shore and two and a quarter hours later, the first landing-craft, packed with Marines, set off for Inchon from the ships that had transported them. On arriving at the beach, they climbed the seawall and started to move inland and, as darkness began to fall, they established themselves ashore. Two regiments of Marines had been landed and there had been only 20 deaths and fewer than 200 casualties. Through the hours of darkness, they awaited a counter-attack but none came. MacArthur had been well and truly vindicated in his assessment of the enemy.

Early the following day, the Marines began to drive eastward, with the capital Seoul their destination. By the following night, they had taken the Kimpo (now Gimpo) airfield and, on 19 September, they swept past the North Korean 18th Division in some heavy fighting and reached the Seoul suburbs.

Break-out from Pusan and the Battle for Seoul

On 16 September, Walker's Eighth Army launched their break-out from the Pusan Perimeter. It was a tortuous business and only three days later did they manage to cross the Naktong in strength. The weather pinned them down for four days but, as it cleared, the bombers moved in and the communists' front began to collapse. Thousands of North Koreans began to retreat, dispensing with weapons and equipment as they did so. The 1st Cavalry, advancing north, met the 7th Infantry, advancing south, at Osan, 22 miles south of Seoul, on 26 September. Meanwhile, on the east coast units of the ROK army were meeting little resistance as they pushed north. The North Koreans were in flight, many surrendering but others melting into the hills from where they would wage guerrilla warfare.

To the north, both regiments of Marines were engaged

in a brutal three-day street battle for Seoul. Later, there would be controversy over the wholesale destruction of the city and the large number of civilian casualties incurred as the North Koreans fought a desperate rearguard action to delay the American advance. Many believed that an enveloping operation, instead of a frontal assault backed up with America's overwhelmingly superior air and artillery support, would have saved lives and property.

At two in the morning of 25 September, the US 5th Marines were given the order to launch an attack. It was no secret that General Almond had promised MacArthur that his men would take the capital by the 25th and this was a blatant attempt to fulfil that promise. The 5th Marines raised the Stars and Stripes over Seoul's Capitol building on 27 September, but, to their great annoyance, were immediately ordered to take it down and run the UN flag up the flagpole instead. They were two days late, but MacArthur had seen to it that the capture of Seoul had been announced in Tokyo on the 25th anyway.

On the 29th MacArthur took part in the ceremony at the Capitol building that celebrated the liberation of Seoul and the return of Syngman Rhee's government. It was held against the wishes of the Joint Chiefs who were reluctant to allow the United States to be associated too closely with the Rhee regime. As one man said: 'If the Inchon landing had been as carefully planned as that ceremony, it would have been marvellous.' But the great man was not to be denied his moment and, in order to make it happen, a large amount of men, resources and time had to be diverted from the fighting to construct a pontoon bridge across the Han River so that his cavalcade could drive direct from Kimpo airfield into the centre of the city.

Syngman Rhee, for his part, was overcome with emotion and immensely grateful to MacArthur for liberating Seoul and restoring him to power. 'We admire you,' he told the general, 'We love you as the saviour of our race.' MacArthur flew back to Tokyo, confident that the war in Korea had been all but won, thanks to him.

Little did he know.

5

Beyond the 38ᵗʰ Parallel

What Next?

The communists had come very close to capturing South Korea, but had eventually been seen off by the United Nations Coalition. July and August had seen humiliating defeats for the forces of the West but the miracle of Inchon wiped away all the bad memories of those opening months of the war. Even better was the realisation that there had been no other communist action anywhere in the world. Western leaders were reassured and filled with renewed confidence. It looked as if the world war that they had been fearing was not going to materialise in Korea, at any rate.

The big question, of course, was what next? Many were of the opinion that Kim Il-sung should not be allowed to get away with his actions and especially the atrocities that his troops had perpetrated on the South Koreans. This, of course, ignored the atrocities that the South Koreans had perpetrated on their own people. At the United Nations in New York, the Soviets, who had resumed their seat on the Security Council in early August, argued that the war in Korea was, in fact, a conflict between two parts of the Korean people who were temporarily split and governed by separate authorities. The questions for the coalition were whether to pursue the North Korean army into its homeland and whether this was actually a legitimate war aim. Many in the US administration believed it was legitimate, while others worried that such an action would almost certainly bring China and/or the Soviet Union into the conflict, creating a bigger war. Furthermore, it was doubtful whether members of the United Nations would be supportive of any such moves. Truman had, thus far, made no decision on future actions. General MacArthur, of course, was not a believer in limited warfare, and was intent on destroying the army of North Korea. In order to do that, it would be necessary to invade and occupy the country.

A National Security Council document, NSC 81, provided a compromise, suggesting that only Republic of Korea troops should cross the 38th Parallel, but this was judged 'unrealistic' by the Joint Chiefs. Eventually, they informed MacArthur that his military objective was the destruction of the North Korean armed forces. He was to be permitted to conduct military operations north of the 38th Parallel as long as neither Soviet nor Chinese forces had entered Korea. It was made very clear to him that in no circumstances should his troops cross the

Manchurian or Russian borders with North Korea and that non-Korean forces were not to be employed in the north-east provinces close to the Soviet or Manchurian borders. He was not to engage in air or naval operations against Manchurian or Soviet territory. None of this, however, was to be made public as it might precipitate a new vote at the United Nations which would inevitably be vetoed by the Soviet Union. A number of America's allies supported an advance across the 38th Parallel, and Britain for one, a vocal member of this group, was eager to extract maximum benefit from recent successes.

MacArthur ordered Walker to say nothing but to prepare his troops. He told the JCS: 'My overall strategic plan is known to you. Unless and until the enemy capitulates, I regard all of Korea open for our military operations.' There were geographical problems with operations in North Korea. The Taebaek mountain range rendered west to east movements of troops impossible and all routes in the north ran north to south along river valleys. But MacArthur, the master of amphibious operations, proposed another strategy. The plan was to transport Almond's force from Inchon by boat to the North Korean port of Wonsan on the country's east coast. From there they would push north towards the Manchurian border while Walker's troops would also advance northwards, from Seoul to Pyongyang. Inevitably, there was opposition to the plan. Walker thought it was pointless to send Almond's men all the way by sea to Wonsan when ROK troops were advancing up the east coast and encountering very little resistance. He was also insulted by MacArthur's decision to continue with the dual command with Almond. Military convention was, after all, to operate under a single, unified authority. The truth was that MacArthur and others doubted Walker's ability but realised it would be destructive to remove him from his command when they were so close to victory.

ROK troops crossed the Parallel on 28 September but the American soldiers, eager to follow and anxious to get this over with so that they could go home before the vicious Korean winter set in, had to wait while diplomacy took its course in Washington. The other members of the UN coalition were getting anxious. The British, especially, were unnerved by what was emerging from Beijing. Even so, the Foreign Secretary, Ernest Bevin (1881-1951), asked that the United Nations might make an appeal to the North Koreans to put down their arms, on the understanding that, if they did not, the Americans would cross the 38th Parallel. The Americans replied that the UN forces were indeed making such an appeal, thus placating the British.

Diplomacy, of course, was not General MacArthur's strong suit. On 8 October, he issued an ultimatum to the North Koreans, informing them that if they did not lay down their arms, he would have no option but to 'at once proceed to take such military action as may be necessary to enforce the decrees of the United Nations'. He had undoubtedly overstepped the mark yet again, ignoring the politicians, the diplomats and the limits of his power and authority. Once again, however, the Truman administration remained silent. The alternative – to dismiss him – especially after the success of Inchon, was unthinkable. It would do too much damage to Truman, the war effort and, ultimately, to the authority of the United States.

A Fateful Meeting

It was apparent in Washington that, by this time in the war, the Russians were having second thoughts. They wanted to dissociate themselves from the North Korean invasion and were anxious to prevent the war from escalating. At the same time, the Americans failed to realise that the Chinese might be thinking very differently to Moscow and might have their own reasons for becoming involved.

Nonetheless, the Eighth Army crossed the 38th Parallel on 9 October and endured a week of hard fighting. All of a sudden, however, the North Koreans retreated, the UN forces following in hot pursuit. It was at this critical moment that Truman requested a meeting with MacArthur on Wake Island, a coral island in the Pacific, roughly halfway between Tokyo and the United States. MacArthur was disgusted by the request which he believed to be nothing more than a PR stunt by the president. Truman claimed that it was time he met the man who was calling the shots in the Far East but the reality was that he was struggling at home, and was viewed as soft on communism. Association with what appeared to be a successful campaign in Korea would, therefore, do him no harm.

Interestingly, when Truman came down the steps of his plane on Wake Island, the general did not salute him, as would be normal for a serving officer. Instead, he shook the president's hand, giving the impression that the two men were equals. It was a contemptuous gesture. But, they talked for an hour, alone in a hut on the edge of the airfield, MacArthur assuring the president that the Chinese would not involve themselves in the Korean conflict. He also assured him that victory was close. Finally, he promised Truman that he harboured no political ambitions, dismissing the speculation that he would be seeking the Republican presidential nomination at some point. They then engaged in a proper meeting involving their entourages. Although no notes were taken at either of these meetings, it is recorded that MacArthur intimated that resistance throughout Korea would be ended by Thanksgiving and that the Eighth Army would be withdrawn by Christmas, leaving General Almond's X Corps as an occupying force. Once again, he discredited the notion of Chinese or Russian involvement in the conflict. In terms of the country's future, he said he supported Syngman Rhee. After MacArthur declined Truman's invitation to lunch, the general was somewhat surprised by a small ceremony at which he was awarded his fifth Distinguished Service medal.

MacArthur was furious to have been summoned in such a way but the meeting was significant because it gave the administration an opportunity to remind the general of his responsibilities, and that he should be following the orders and the policies of his government. As ever, MacArthur cast his charismatic spell over the government delegation to the extent that they were somewhat in awe of him. The failure to pursue a proper agenda at Wake and to effectively deal with the general was a serious mistake by Truman and it would colour his conduct of the war in the months to come.

Advancing on All Fronts

The North Korean capital fell to the 10,000-strong 1st ROK Division, commanded by General Paik Sun-yup (b. 1920) on 19 October but, by this time, Pyongyang was a ghost town. Its inhabitants had fled or gone into hiding. As for Kim Il-sung, he had escaped into the mountains to the north. The Americans selected a council of what they termed 'representative non-American citizens' to take over the day-to-day running of the city. It appeared as if the war was over. North Korean troops had simply melted away, abandoning their weapons and equipment. An intelligence briefing was issued throughout Far East Command by MacArthur's long-time Chief of Intelligence, Colonel Charles A Willoughby (1892-1972):

'Organized resistance on any large scale has ceased to be an enemy capability. Indications are that the North Korean military and political headquarters may have fled into Manchuria. Communications with, and consequent control of, the enemy's field units have dissipated to a point of ineffectiveness. In spite of these indications of disorganization, there are no signs, at the moment, that the enemy intends to surrender. He continues to retain the capability of fighting small scale delaying actions against UN pressure...'

Meanwhile X Corps was on the water, heading for Wonsan but was seriously delayed by mines at the entrance to the harbour. The force was embarrassed to find that, when they eventually made landfall, the ROK troops were already there. The ROK 3rd and Capital Divisions had arrived in the port on 10 October, having hastened north from the 38th Parallel in two weeks. In fact, the Capital Division was 50 miles north of Wonsan by the time the Americans arrived. Even the comedian, Bob Hope, had beaten them to it and had performed his show the night before they landed.

The US Eighth Army were at that moment on a triumphant drive north towards the Yalu River which formed the border with China. Around this time, the British put forward a plan for a buffer zone south of the Yalu that would be controlled by the Chinese and the United Nations. An outraged MacArthur compared it to Chamberlain's meeting and agreement with Adolf

Hitler at Munich in 1938. Rather extravagantly, he said such an action would be 'the greatest defeat of the free world in recent times'. Instead, on 20 October, he ordered everyone to prepare to advance to the northern North Korean border and a new order four days later took away all restrictions on US troops advancing all the way to the Yalu. In effect, he was disobeying his orders from the Joint Chiefs. He also refused to give assurances that he would declare the Chinese power station at Suiho protected against UN forces. The JCS believed the war to be almost over and, for that reason, once again failed to confront MacArthur.

And so MacArthur got his way once again. His UNC troops forged north without any political considerations. The advance proceeded without any kind of debate, military expediency – the prospect of victory, that is – superseding everything. Triumphalism was prevalent in Washington and elsewhere.

At last those communists were being taken on.

6

Chinese Intervention

Doubt and Disbelief

The South Korean army reached the Yalu on 25 October, but that day ROK II Corps was attacked by what they believed to be Chinese troops. To prove that it had, indeed, been the Chinese, they sent some prisoners to the Americans but, even after one of the prisoners admitted that there were many Chinese in Korea, the Americans still refused to believe it. MacArthur and his men in Tokyo did not believe the stories of Chinese soldiers fighting on the peninsula. General Walker explained it away simplistically, saying that just as there are many Mexicans living in Texas, the same was probably true for Chinese in the north of North Korea. But the ROK and UN forces began to experience reverses. The ROK 1st Division, engaged in battle at the Chosin Reservoir, took a number of prisoners who turned out to be Chinese. The Argyll & Sutherland Highlanders of the 27th Brigade encountered strangely dressed troops in a skirmish close to the Chongchon River, north of Pyongyang. When the Argylls examined the bodies of the enemy, they found them to be wearing padded clothing of the style worn by the Chinese, and one was found to be wearing a peaked cap with a red star badge on it.

The Chinese would not launch their main assault for another three weeks but they were evidently already in Korea, causing significant damage between 1 and 3 November. On the evening of 1 November, they hit a unit of the 8th Cavalry at Ansung (now Anseong) southeast of Seoul. It was reported by a patrol of F Company that they were under attack by unknown troops that their South Korean colleagues identified as speaking Chinese. At Ansung, the 3rd Battalion of the 8th Cavalry was wiped out by a Chinese force and other battalions were also badly hit. But just as suddenly as they had appeared, the Chinese disappeared again and the fighting returned to little more than local skirmishes.

MacArthur and his men in Tokyo continued to pay little heed to stories of Chinese soldiers fighting in Korea even though all the intelligence suggested otherwise. The CIA speculated that there were 40,000 Chinese troops in Korea, but that, across the border, around 700,000 were massing, ready to attack. Still Washington persisted in the belief that China would not act alone, without the support of the Soviet Union, and that the Russians most decidedly did not want any escalation in the war.

The general feeling in Washington was that they

should find out just how serious the Chinese were; to call their bluff, in fact. It seems evident that the Chinese were reluctant at first to engage fully with the war. Perhaps those early skirmishes were merely tests, to see just how good the UN troops were. Finding that they could beat them, they would have been encouraged. They would also have been concerned that, unless the UN forces were defeated, they would, indeed, advance all the way to the Yalu and the Chinese border.

It was not the ideal time for China to engage in a war. It had only a few years earlier come to the end of a very damaging 22-year-long civil war. The country had suffered natural disasters in 1949 which affected 40 million Chinese; there was unrest in the cities; and there was opposition to Chairman Mao's land reform policies. All the while, the existence of nationalist Formosa was a constant irritation to the Chinese communists. But the vast manpower of China's army – around 5 million men – was at the same time being dismantled and sent back to where it was most needed – to China's farms and factories.

Although Chinese railways played a major role in transporting equipment and supplies from Russia to North Korea, it cannot be said that they had any influence over Kim's decision to invade the Republic of Korea. Indeed, many senior figures were well aware of the inadequacies of the People's Liberation Army – in essence still a guerrilla army, following the civil war. What did really affect China was Truman's announcement that Chinese occupation of Formosa would be a threat to the security of the Pacific region and to United States forces operating there. They took the blockade of the strait between Formosa and China more seriously than the American and UN intervention in Korea. America's growing friendship with Chiang's Formosa was disturbing for the Chinese. They were further alarmed, therefore, by the prospect of American troops on one bank of the Yalu, looking across at China on the other bank.

In the autumn of 1950, anti-American propaganda began to be broadcast and printed in China, and in statements and in private conversations with dignitaries such as the Indian ambassador to China, the Chinese expressed their unhappiness with events in Korea. General Nieh Jung-chen (1899-1992) told the ambassador that the Chinese would not sit back and watch the Americans come right up to their borders.

'...at all costs American aggression has got to be stopped. The Americans can bomb us, they can destroy our industries, but they cannot defeat us on land... We have calculated all that... They may even drop atom bombs on us. What then? They may kill a few million people. Without sacrifice, a nation's independence cannot be upheld... After all, China lives on the farms. What can atom bombs do there?'

On 2 October, the Indian ambassador was informed by Chinese premier Zhou Enlai that if the forces of the

United Nations were to cross the 38th Parallel, China would not hesitate to intervene in the war, a claim dismissed by Washington as an empty threat, an attempt to blackmail the UN. One of the problems inherent in these types of statements was, of course, that there were no diplomatic relations between Washington and Beijing which meant a total lack of communication. Five days after Zhou's threat, American troops crossed the 38th Parallel and an order was issued by Mao Zedong to his Chinese People's Volunteers to 'resist the attacks of United States imperialism'. The Chinese 4th Field Army entered Korea a week later, led by Marshal Peng Dehuai (1898-1974). The first Chinese troops in Korea were XIII Army Group. It was made up of four armies that each had three divisions of 10,000 infantrymen, a regiment of cavalry and five artillery regiments. They crossed the bridges on the Yalu under cover of darkness and, incredibly, the UN force had no idea that 130,000 soldiers and support troops were on the move between 13 and 25 October. The Chinese were masters of camouflage but they also eschewed the normal trappings of military movement; there was no unusual radio traffic, there were no trucks and they did not leave supply dumps that would have indicated that a large force was being resupplied.

On the night of 5 November, the Chinese withdrew after making life very difficult for the UN troops along the front. It may have been that they were experiencing problems in supplying their troops, or that they had merely wanted their attacks to serve as a warning to the Americans. They have said that they withdrew in order to 'encourage the enemy's arrogance'. For his part, MacArthur believed that the Chinese had tried their hardest to force the Americans back, but had manifestly failed. He ordered that the drive to the Yalu River be resumed.

The Chinese soldiers fighting in Korea were amongst the toughest in the world, many of them having known nothing but war for much of their lives. They had the strength to march or even run for mile upon mile and could live on minimal rations. A Chinese soldier, it was said, could live on eight to ten pounds of supply a day, whereas a UNC soldier needed 60. This gave them a huge logistical advantage. What supplies they did require were carried by tens of thousands of porters lugging 80 to 100 pounds on a pole across their shoulders or on an A-frame. Uniforms were of quilted cotton and they wore tennis shoes on their feet. Most were driven by the spirit of revolution, the knowledge that Mao's revolution had ended the autocratic landlordism and endemic corruption that had blighted their homeland for centuries.

But, by 15 November, after four-and-a-half months of war, 135,000 North Korean prisoners of war had been taken and it was estimated that there had been 335,000 North Korean casualties. Troops still hung on to the promise made by MacArthur that they would be home for Christmas and vehicles and equipment were even being cleaned, ready for shipment back to Japan or the United States.

Withdrawal Becomes Flight

On 25 November, General Walker's Eighth Army and General Almond's X Corps began to advance once more but they soon encountered the Chinese. Fighting erupted along the length of the Chongchon Valley, the terrifying cacophony of sounds with which the Americans would become familiar echoing into the night – bugles, drums, rattles and whistles. The Chinese attacked again and again, overrunning the American positions and forcing them to pull back two miles down the valley. The Americans performed badly again, stunned by these attacks and failing to respond effectively. They were also appalled by the waves of almost suicidal Chinese troops who did not seem to value life. It engendered panic and disorganisation.

Worse still was happening on the Eighth Army's right flank where ROK II Corps, a force made up of three divisions of men, had fallen apart during the night, the soldiers fleeing, as usual abandoning weapons and equipment. This left a yawning gap in the UN line some 80 miles wide. With his forces in danger of being cut off, Walker ordered them to retreat, moving down the west coast to Sukchon and Pyongyang, creating a 50-mile traffic jam. Meanwhile, at Kunu-ri (now Kunu-dong), the artillery of 2nd Infantry Division, commanded by Major General Laurence B Keiser (1895-1969), was covering the withdrawal across the Chongchon River of I Corps and 25th Division.

By 28 November, even MacArthur had to acknowledge that the withdrawal had turned into a flight. He sent a message to the United Nations:

'Enemy reactions developed in the course of our assault operations of the past four days disclose that a major segment of the Chinese continental forces in army, corps and divisional organization of an aggregate strength of over 200,000 men is now arrayed against the United Nations forces in North Korea... Consequently, we face an entirely new war.'

The Pentagon was concerned about the coordination of the retreat of the Eighth Army with X Corps. Finally, on 30 November, MacArthur received orders to withdraw Almond's X Corps from north-east Korea as it was in an exposed position. This withdrawal was to be coordinated with that of the Eighth Army so that the enemy was unable to outflank them or cut between the two forces. In essence, the Joint Chiefs of Staff were insisting that the two forces be unified under one command in a line of defence across the Korean peninsula. The days of two commands were over.

A strategy of X Corps striking at the Chinese rear did not go well when they came under heavy artillery fire and the Chinese took Songchon on the east–west Pyongyang–Wonsan road. MacArthur decided the only course was to pull out, outrunning the pursuing Chinese, stretching their supply lines and making them vulnerable to attack from the air. He now became political, blaming his failure to hold the line across the centre of Korea not just on the terrain, the logistical problems or his lack of sufficient forces but on Washington and its insistence on limiting the hostilities to Korea. It was 'without precedent in military history,' MacArthur complained. The situation was becoming worse and, within a week of launching the offensive that they believed would win the war, the Allied forces were now contemplating whether they would have to get out of Korea altogether.

On 5 December, Pyongyang, to date the only communist capital ever to fall into Western hands, was evacuated. As the Allied troops headed southwards, they could see great pillars of flame and smoke, rising from supply dumps that had been torched to prevent them from falling into enemy hands. The return of the Chinese army and Kim Il-sung to the decimated city was anticipated. The former conquerors of the capital made their way south to the 38th Parallel as swiftly as possible, followed by a long train of refugees. They had lost 11,000 casualties, dead, wounded or missing, in the first days of the Chinese presence in Korea. It was one of the worst moments in American military history.

The 1st Marine Division was, meanwhile, trapped at the Chosin Reservoir, some 78 miles north of the port city of Hungnam on the east coast of North Korea. On the 27th, they had started clearing the road that led westwards but that night, the Marines faced heavy fighting, and were attacked from the front as well as on the main supply route south. By the following morning, the Marines had been split into three isolated perimeters, at Yudam-ni, Hagaru-ri and Koto-ri, by these assaults, and the Chinese had reached as far as Chinhung-ni, 37 miles south of Yudam-ni. The Marines now faced the 12 divisions of the IX Army Group.

The Marines held their positions in the face of heavy fighting. Hagaru-ri was of critical importance as it had the airbase from which the regiments at Yudam-ni would have to withdraw. On 1 December, around 10,000 US troops set out on the perilous 14-mile march to Hagaru-ri, arriving by 4 December. Operating under X Corps was a 1,000-man relief force, made up of Marines, US Army troops and British Royal Marine Commandos of 41st Independent Commando who had set out for Hagaru-ri on 29 November to reinforce the Hagaru-ri Perimeter. They were known as Task Force Drysdale, named for the Royal Marine Lieutenant Colonel Douglas B Drysdale (1917-90). It was a tortuous advance north, under constant fire, but supported by a company of tanks. Having travelled only four miles by nightfall, it was decided to proceed under cover of darkness.

The column was ambushed by the Chinese in a gorge that had been dubbed 'Hellfire Alley', just five miles from where they had set out. Some of the US Army personnel had little stomach for the fight and returned to Koto-ri, while some American Marines and British Commandos fought throughout the night. Many surrendered but some made it through to Hagaru-ri, suffering from frostbite. Task Force Drysdale suffered 321 casualties, 61 of them British Marines; 71 vehicles were destroyed. What remained of 41 Commando took over at Hagaru-ri, keeping this vital base and airstrip safe.

A Difficult Winter

At Hagaru-ri, temperatures could plummet during the winter months to as low as -20 degrees. The simplest action was difficult in such cold and vehicles had to be kept running constantly so that their engines would not seize up. Blood plasma froze and orderlies had to carry syrettes of morphine in their mouths to stop them freezing. In the meantime, of course, the fighting continued. The days were relatively quiet, but at night the bugles, whistles and ghoulish screams and yells would start and the communists would throw themselves at the Allied troops. It was a terrifying experience and men were even forbidden to zip their sleeping bags closed for fear of being trapped in them and bayoneted. 'Warming tents' were introduced behind the lines so that every few hours men could go and thaw themselves out to be better equipped to deal with the enemy.

Task Force Faith – 2,500 infantry, artillery and tank units from the 7th Infantry Division – had been fighting at the Chosin Reservoir as part of what was called the 'Home-by-Christmas Offensive'. Their mission was to guard the east flank of the 1st Marine Division which was attacking north-west from the reservoir. They had occupied the east side of the reservoir. Not anticipating any enemy activity, when they arrived in their position on 27 November they failed to set up a tight perimeter. The Chinese launched a surprise attack during the night, inflicting heavy casualties on the Americans and forcing them to cancel their offensive. Reinforcements failed to arrive and they were surrounded and cut off. The Chinese attacked again the following night in falling snow and punishing temperatures that plunged as low as -30. It was so cold that several US soldiers froze to death in their foxholes. As the task force attempted to withdraw the following day, Marine aircraft struck the communists with a heavy bombardment of napalm, rockets and fragmentation bombs. With more than half their number dead, and running low on ammunition, the Allied force had little option but to try to break out to the Marine lines to the south on 1 December. Weighed down with hundreds of wounded and under constant attack, they suffered friendly fire incidents, losing more of their number. By that night, almost all the officers were dead or wounded.

After attacking Hill 1221, overlooking the road, many soldiers did not return to the column of trucks, instead continuing onto the frozen reservoir behind the hill and walking on the ice in the direction of the Marine positions that were several miles to the south. In the dark, the column of trucks started to move slowly again, but faced another Chinese roadblock north of Hudong. Tanks and troops who had been based there had been ordered back to Hagaru-ri the previous day, an order that remains controversial to this day. The Chinese attacked again and the leader of the task force, Lieutenant Colonel Don C Faith Jr (1918-50) was killed. The troops abandoned the truck convoy and fled, many going on to the reservoir ice. Many members of Task Force Faith managed to escape but, of the original 2,500, more than 1,000 died and 300 were captured. Of the thousand or so survivors who reached Hagaru-ri, only 385 were judged to be in a fit state to take their place in the line.

Ironically, General Almond had flown into the area by helicopter on 27 November to announce that, 'We're still attacking and we're going all the way to the Yalu.' He added, 'Don't let a bunch of Chinese laundrymen stop you.' Soon, however, it became apparent that those 'Chinese laundrymen' were wreaking havoc around the Chosin Reservoir.

7

The End of the Road for MacArthur

The Ridgway Effect

At the beginning of 1951, the UN Coalition was still on the back foot and, just a week before the New Year, an event occurred that would change the entire course of the war. On 23 December, General Walton Walker was killed in a collision between his jeep and an ROK truck. By the time of his death, Walker, who had been so successful with the Pusan Perimeter, was exhausted. After many disputes with Almond, and the poor performance of his Eighth Army, he had believed that MacArthur was about to replace him. Now MacArthur was forced to find a new man to lead the Eighth Army. His choice of successor was 56-year-old General Matthew Ridgway (1895-1993) who had commanded with distinction the 82nd Airborne Division in Sicily, Italy and Normandy during the Second World War. Generally regarded as one of the outstanding US commanders of the war, he was noted for wearing a first-aid kit and a grenade on his shoulder straps and was said to have often stood urinating in the middle of a road under artillery fire during the Second World War to show his contempt for the accuracy of German fire. On his arrival in Korea, Ridgway's initial optimism soon dissipated after speaking to his troops:

'I had discovered that our forces were simply not mentally and spiritually ready for the sort of action I had been planning... The men I met along the road, those I stopped to talk to and to solicit gripes from – they too all conveyed to me a conviction that this was a bewildered army, not sure of itself or its leaders, not sure what they were doing there, wondering when they would hear the whistle of that homebound transport.'

Ridgway was disappointed by the low morale of the troops now under his command, and by the prevailing notion that the only way forward was to evacuate UNC forces from Korea. He was equally dismayed by the inadequacies of equipment and winter clothing. The food being served up to his troops was poor and there was a distinct lack of leadership. Troops, he found, were given no information as to their purpose in Korea and were in sore need of proper training. So, he began to effect immediate change in the Eighth Army. Tighter discipline was instilled in the men who were encouraged to take better care of their equipment and their vehicles. It appeared that the irrepressible Ridgway had arrived just in time, although it took him a little while to establish his ideas.

The bitter cold of a Korean winter was in full swing as 1951 arrived. Both sides were inadequately equipped for the rigours of the season. Some Chinese soldiers did not even have boots and Chinese captives reported that around 50 per cent of the troops in the Chinese front line were affected by frostbite. As ever, the supply line issue loomed large for the Chinese and it was acknowledged that the deeper into South Korea they penetrated, the more difficult it was to supply them. Nonetheless, Mao Zedong was keen for his army to recapture Seoul. His general, Peng Dehuai, however, wanted to stop just north of the Parallel and winter for a few months. Mao inevitably won the argument and the Third Phase Offensive was launched on New Year's Eve, Chinese troops initially enjoying some success. As ever, attacks were sound-tracked by disquieting trumpets and gongs, panicking some UN troops and putting them to flight. The UNC forces were overwhelmed and the Chinese and North Koreans retook Seoul four days into 1951.

From MacArthur's base in the Dai Ichi in Tokyo there now emerged a series of gloomy reports, greatly exaggerating the number of Chinese troops in Korea and intimating that the war could not be won. Meanwhile, MacArthur continued to press his political superiors and the JCS to allow him to bomb the bridges across the Yalu and across the border into China. Perhaps as a response to MacArthur's straining at the leash, Truman issued an order to all US commanders to show 'extreme caution' in their public communications. All such pronouncements were first to be cleared with the State Department. Needless to say, MacArthur ignored these orders. He went as far as to indicate that were he to continue to operate under the restraints imposed upon him by Washington, he would be forced to evacuate all troops from the Korean peninsula.

Washington refused to comply and, in fact, on 29 December, he was told by the JCS that there would be no more reinforcements and that the administration did not want a major war in Korea. Indeed, they said, if an evacuation became necessary, then so be it. MacArthur's response took the form of four demands – a blockade of the Chinese coast; permission to bomb Chinese industrial establishments; the reinforcement of his force with Chinese nationalist troops; and all restrictions on Chiang Kai-shek's troops to be lifted, allowing Nationalist China to attack the People's Republic of China. MacArthur was convinced that this was what was needed to defeat China, but once again his ideas were rejected by his superiors.

In truth, there had been a subtle change in policy in Washington and at the United Nations, one that MacArthur had suspected. No longer was it believed that the original aim of a unified, non-communist Korea could be achieved. The objective now was to enjoy sufficient military success to persuade North Korea and China to the negotiating table so that a return to the status quo of pre-war Korea could be discussed. From the spring of 1951 until the end of 1953, it was a matter of killing as many North Koreans and Chinese as possible, while taking acceptable losses, and defending enough territory to secure a peaceful resolution to the conflict.

But, in the first few weeks of 1951, Ridgway was beginning to make some progress, even though his UN force of 365,000 troops was still outnumbered by around 486,000 – of whom some 350,000 were Chinese. In addition, it was estimated that there were another 400,000 troops being held in reserve in Manchuria. Ridgway advanced, meeting little resistance in mid-January as his troops reached Suwon in the west, Wonju in the middle of the country and Samcheok in the east. By late January, the People's Volunteer Army had abandoned its lines and Ridgway launched his first offensive, Operation Thunderbolt, on 25 January. It resulted in the retreat of the Chinese 38th and 50th Armies and, by 9 February, the UNC had recaptured Inchon and Suwon. Ridgway lost 70 men, but the Chinese suffered more than 4,000 casualties. His men continued their advance towards the Han River.

To the east there was heavy fighting at Chipyong-ni (now Jipyeong-ri) but air power did untold damage to the waves of Chinese troops that were thrown at the American lines and the Americans held on. This battle, in which the Americans were outnumbered some fifteen to one, is sometimes dubbed the Gettysburg of the Korean War as it was something of a turning point. The Americans had performed well and morale was vastly improved.

The Chinese offensive had hit the buffers which marked an important moment for the United Nations Coalition. They had withstood the fiercest offensive yet from the Chinese and UN troops began to realise that the enemy could be defeated. As a British officer, Air Vice-Marshal Cecil Bouchier (1895-1979) excitedly reported back to Britain:

'The myth of the magical millions of the Chinese in Korea has been exploded. In the last United Nations offensive, the Americans have learned how easy it is to kill the Chinese, and their morale has greatly increased thereby.'

Ridgway launched Operation Killer on 21 February and, by 1 March, the Chinese were retreating, suffering huge casualties. He now had seven American divisions advancing in line, defending in depth while their massive air power and artillery rained down on Chinese positions ahead. In Operation Ripper that followed, his troops surrounded Seoul and the Chinese rapidly fled from the capital. He had made this action work by dissuading MacArthur from coming to launch the offensive – and at the same time grab a few photo opportunities, thereby alerting the enemy that something was afoot. The capital the Americans recaptured on 14 March, however, was a scene of devastation, and, of its important buildings, only the Capitol building and the railway station had survived intact. Unfortunately, the enemy in full flight was allowed to escape at Munsan and another daring escape was effected by the North Korean 10th Division which had been fighting a guerrilla war in the south since the turn of the year. They smashed through the ROK lines near Kangnung (now Gangneung).

On 27 March, UN troops – ROK I Corps – crossed the 38th Parallel, and took the town of Yangyang four days later. The Americans were also advancing northwards, aiming to reach the area known as the 'Iron Triangle' that was bounded by the counties of Chorwon, Kumhwa and Pyongyang. Situated south of the capital, Pyongyang, the Iron Triangle contained the major rail and road links between the north-eastern port of Wonsan and Seoul. It was vital, therefore to the North Korean supply system. By 9 April, UNC forces had arrived at what was known as the Kansas Line, marked by the Imjin River to the west and the Hwachon Reservoir in the centre. Another line – the Wyoming Line – was demarcated to the north and it was planned that I and IX should advance towards it.

Meanwhile, storm clouds were gathering in Washington. Truman had had his fill of the recalcitrant general in the Dai ichi.

The End for MacArthur

It was inherently distasteful to Americans to be struggling so much to defeat the communists in Asia.

They had, after all, just won a global war, using all the technological and military power they could amass, including the use of the ultimate weapon, the atomic bomb. But now, the richest and most powerful country in the world was unable to force her will upon a much weaker enemy and, to make matters worse, American troops were dying in their thousands in the conflict. All of this was anathema to the right wing of the Republican Party that was increasing in influence in the US political arena. They believed that the American military should be allowed to employ its vast technological advantage to bring the war to a conclusion. This meant not excluding the use of nuclear weapons, if that was the only way.

Meanwhile, MacArthur continued to try to exert pressure on the administration. He spoke of large air attacks to isolate North Korea from China and, somewhat implausibly, suggested the establishment of a boundary between the forces of communism and 'freedom' by creating a no-man's-land that was seeded with radioactive waste. Truman, on the other hand, as we have seen, was keen to start talking about a ceasefire. MacArthur, of course, could not accept this and anti-Washington, as well as anti-communist, propaganda began to flow relentlessly from the Dai Ichi. Much of the ire was directed at America's allies who, to MacArthur's eyes, were weak and ineffectual. He even drummed up a theory that the British had tried to persuade Washington to give China the seat occupied by Chiang Kai-shek at the United Nations.

The British, for their part, continued to be concerned about MacArthur and were very worried about what he might do. This contributed to the desire in Washington to take action. The British Foreign Secretary, Herbert Morrison (1888-1965), discussed the concern about MacArthur in a cable to the British Ambassador in Washington, Sir Oliver Franks (1905-92):

'Our principal difficulty is General MacArthur. His policy is different from the policy of the UN. He seems to want a war with China. We do not. It is no exaggeration to say that by his public utterances, he has weakened public confidence in this country and in Western Europe in the quality of American political judgement and leadership. Here we seem to have a case of a commander publicly suggesting that his policy is not the stated policy of his government, not subject to the control of his own government, and whom his own government is, nevertheless, unwilling and unable to discipline.'

Little did he know as he was writing this cable that Truman had already made up his mind that MacArthur had to go. On 5 April, in the House of Representatives, Representative Joe Martin (1884-1968) read a letter he had received from MacArthur in answer to a request from Martin that the general comment upon the idea of allowing Chiang's troops to land on mainland China. MacArthur had written:

'It seems strangely difficult for some to realise that here in Asia is where the Communist conspirators have elected to make their play for global conquest, and that we have joined the issue thus raised on the battlefield; that here we fight Europe's war with arms while the diplomats there still fight it with words; that if we lose this war to Communism in Asia the fall of Europe is inevitable; win it and Europe most probably would avoid war and yet preserve freedom. As you have pointed out, we must win. There is no substitute for victory...'

The divergence in positions between MacArthur and the administration was apparent to all. As one senator remarked, the United States now had two foreign policies – 'that of General MacArthur and that of the President'. Speculation mounted in the media that the general would be dismissed but several of Truman's advisers hesitated. Nonetheless, the president asked for the opinion of the Joint Chiefs of Staff and they confirmed his view that the general should be relieved of his position but 'on purely military considerations'.

The order for MacArthur's dismissal and the promotion of General Matthew Ridgway to his position was made public on 11 April in a statement by President Truman, part of which read:

'With deep regret I have concluded that General of the Army Douglas MacArthur is unable to give his wholehearted support to the policies of the United States government and of the United Nations in matters pertaining to his official duties. In view of the specific responsibility imposed on me by the Constitution of the United States, and of the added responsibility which has been entrusted to me by the United Nations, I have decided that I must make a change of command in the Far East. I have, therefore, relieved General MacArthur of his commands, and have designated Lieutenant General Matthew B. Ridgway as his successor.'

Truman later said:

'I fired him because he wouldn't respect the authority of the President. I didn't fire him because he was a dumb son-of-a-bitch, although he was, but that's not against the law for generals. If it was, half to three-quarters of them would be in jail.'

The decision was greeted with shock in the United States at large and polls suggested that an overwhelming percentage of the public disapproved. By the end of the year, Truman's poll ratings had slipped to 22 per cent, to this day the lowest Gallup Poll rating of any serving president. But it must be remembered that the decision to dismiss MacArthur was taken by a group of the twentieth century's most distinguished military men. And, of course, MacArthur had, to a large extent, brought it on himself. His arrogance knew no bounds and he even flew into Korea on 20 February, following the success of Operation Ripper, claiming to the gathered press that the idea for the operation was his and his alone. In the end, however, it was not just his hubris that got him sacked; it was also his burning ambition to widen the scope of the war by taking it into China, thus creating the very real danger of a global war.

The actual breaking of the news of his dismissal to MacArthur was handled badly. A signal from General Bradley was delivered to him around 3pm on 11 April but arrived minutes after the world learned of it. MacArthur was naturally very upset, leaving Tokyo for Washington on 16 April amid emotional scenes among his staff and the Japanese people who still felt they owed him a great deal.

In America, he was given ticker-tape parades and was permitted to address Congress, defending his side of the argument over the conduct of the Korean War. This was followed by a speaking tour that excoriated Truman's administration for what MacArthur described as his 'appeasement in Asia and for mismanaging the economy'. Many thought he would seek the Republican presidential nomination, but he did not campaign, hoping that a deadlock between the two candidates, Senator Robert A Taft (1889-1953) and General Dwight D Eisenhower (1890-1969) would open the door for him as a compromise candidate. In the end, the nomination was won by Eisenhower who went on to win the 1952 election by a landslide.

Abroad, the reaction to the general's dismissal was entirely positive and was welcomed with great relief. He had represented to other nations the threat of nuclear war, especially in Europe. They were delighted to see Ridgway replace MacArthur and his position as commander of the Eighth Army was taken by General James Van Fleet (1892-1992) who also seemed eminently suitable for the role. He had commanded in both the First and the Second World Wars. President Truman later said of him: 'General Van Fleet is the greatest general we ever had... I sent him to Greece and he won the war. I sent him to Korea and he won the war.' Van Fleet was asked at his first press conference what his goal in Korea was. He replied, 'I don't know. The answer must come from higher authority.' And above him Ridgway did not disappoint, proving himself an excellent supreme commander. He possessed not just the military skills the role demanded, but also the political judgement and discretion that MacArthur had so badly lacked. He shared with MacArthur the inability to get the United States out of Korea but he did not believe Korea to be the place to launch a major war and at no point was there any question about his loyalty to and respect for his superiors.

The Battle of the Imjin River

Van Fleet was not given much time to settle into his new role. On the same day as his press conference, Sunday 22 April 1951, the Chinese launched their fifth offensive of the conflict. They were ordered by General Peng to make maximum use of the transport available, including captured American vehicles. There were to be around 500,000 troops available and much of the attacking was to be undertaken at night. In Peng's sights were three divisions of US troops, three brigades of British and Turkish troops and two divisions of troops of the Republic of Korea. But the Eighth Army's intelligence was good and Van Fleet was fully aware that the attack was imminent, believing that it would take place around the Imjin River, in the Pakyong-Chunchon (now Chuncheon) area in the centre of the front line where IX Corps were based. The Chinese were attempting to halt the Allies' advance towards the Kansas Line around the 38th Parallel which had been going on for about three weeks. The British soldiers of the Glosters and the Northumberland Fusiliers were soon hemmed in by savage fighting. On 21 April, a small reconnaissance force was beaten off but the following day the Chinese offensive was launched in earnest. The orders from Van Fleet were to hold the Kansas Line at whatever cost. Van Fleet was intent on his troops putting up robust resistance to the Chinese onslaught, but also accepted that this would mean higher casualties. To withdraw would have been a blow to the good morale that Ridgway had so carefully cultivated in the previous months.

By 25 April, the Glosters were surrounded and cut off on the hill known as Hill 325. Ammunition was running low and a relief operation had to be called off. They were reduced to a fighting force of about 440 to 450 men, facing an enemy estimated to have consisted of something between a regiment (three battalions) and a division (three regiments). Chinese troops were by now infiltrating far beyond the line, leading to the decision to withdraw to Line Delta. The Glosters were given permission to break out at 6.05am and had no option but to leave behind around 100 wounded. Those who made it out successfully split into small groups to try to avoid the Chinese who were surrounding them. Only 63 men made it to the UN lines. UNC casualties amounted to 1,091 in the three days of fierce fighting at the Imjin River and 622 officers and men lost their lives. Van Fleet felt that the loss of the 622 saved many times that number of troops and that the Glosters' courageous sacrifice had delayed the advance of the Chinese 64th and 65th armies. Marshal Peng was forced to stop his advance and reorganise his troops.

At the same time as the Glosters were being wiped out on the Imjin, Van Fleet was attempting to create a reserve position north of Seoul, known as the 'No Name Line'. There, the Eighth Army easily held off the communists who, by this time, were exhausted. Their exhaustion, however, did not stop their commanders and a new offensive was launched by Marshal Peng on 15 May, involving 21 Chinese and 9 North Korean divisions. The troops of the ROK III collapsed, as ROK troops had been doing throughout the fighting so far, and the communists advanced up to 30 miles. Bucking the trend, though, the ROK I Corps held its line on the right flank, sustaining 900 casualties in the process. The US 2nd Division also held its line, while the 38th Infantry, on the night of 16 May, fought off fierce and relentless communist attacks. The slaughter was horrific, as recorded by the divisional history of the Second Indianhead Division:

'Artillery, crashing into the ground forward of the lines, took a terrific toll of the attackers while other hundreds died in the minefields checkered with barbed wire. The groans of the wounded, screams of the attackers and the blast of bugles mingled with the clattering roar of battle as waves of Chinese pushed against the lines... Searchlights were turned on to illuminate the battle area and aid the defenders in locating and slaughtering the onrushing Chinese.'

Even with reserves of more than 300,000 men, Peng realised around this time that the offensive was proving unsuccessful, although not because of the UNC advance; rather, it was because of his army's huge losses of both men and equipment. The communists had suffered an estimated 90,000 casualties. Meanwhile, American reinforcements added to his difficulties and he had no option but to abandon the offensive for the time being. Van Fleet seized that moment to launch a counter-offensive, regaining lost ground such as the Imjin Line and reaching Kansong (now Gansong) and as far as the Hwachon Reservoir. A strategic retreat was made and thus was brought to an end the frantic and often savage fighting that had marked the first 11 months of the conflict.

8

Stalemate

Aiming for Attrition and Settlement

The communists were devastated and there was an opportunity, had the political will existed, for the UNC to advance even further northwards. The risk, however, was too great. Instead, the Joint Chiefs announced that their objective was now to work towards 'an end to the fighting, and a return to the status quo; the mission of the Eighth Army was to inflict enough attrition on the foe to induce him to settle on these terms.' In other words, the conflict had arrived at a kind of stalemate. Van Fleet consolidated his positions, gaining Chorwon and Kumhwa which represented the bottom line of the 'Iron Triangle'. Meanwhile, X Corps cleared out the Haean Basin, known as 'the Punchbowl', which lay several miles south of the 38th Parallel and which had been a stronghold of the communist forces. The front occasionally moved a few miles here and there in the next two years, but that is more or less where it remained for the duration of the war.

Bombing of North Korea continued unabated and UN forces sought to take back all of South Korea while, at the same time, holding on to all the territory they had. Artillery shells continued to fall along the front, the American advantage in firepower continuing to give them the edge. But in the south, the North Koreans waged guerrilla warfare in the autumn of 1951, and Van Fleet ordered Major General Paik Sun-yup to bring it to an end. There were many important battles during this period of stalemate – the battles of Bloody Ridge, Heartbreak Ridge, Pork Chop Hill and Kumsong, to name but a few. The Chinese People's Volunteer Army was troubled by a lack of proper equipment, overextended supply lines and the UN bombers and, consequently, incurred a very high casualty rate.

In November 1951, a conference, held in Shenyang, China, to discuss the logistical issues the Chinese army was facing, decided to speed up the construction of railway lines and airfields, to provide more trucks and to improve defences against the bombers. It made little difference. General Peng consistently demanded more resources, convinced that this was a war where victory was not going to come for either side any time soon. At a further meeting at which the logistical problems were being discussed, government officials complained that they could not adequately fulfil the requirements of the war, Peng exploded, saying angrily:

'You have this and that problem... You should go to the front and see with your own eyes what food and clothing the soldiers have! Not to speak of the casualties! For what are they giving their lives? We have no aircraft. We have only a few guns. Transports are not protected. More and more soldiers are dying of starvation. Can't you overcome some of your difficulties?'

Amidst a great deal of tension, the meeting had to be adjourned by Zhou Enlai. They decided to change tack, to send the army to North Korea in shifts; to speed up the training of Chinese pilots; to buy more military equipment from the Soviet Union; to provide more and better food and clothing; and to move the responsibility for logistics from the army to the central government.

The Chinese, having failed to break through Van Fleet's re-energised Eighth Army, knew that they had reached stalemate. After the stunning victories of their early forays, they were now only able to record small, local successes against the feeble ROK. The cost in both men and resources was crippling to the Chinese economy, especially as they had to pay the Russians for the weapons and ammunition they had provided for the North Koreans. As for the West, it had proved that it was willing to accept any cost to protect Korea, but, for the USA, it had been difficult. Her relationship with the nations that had joined the coalition had endured a great deal of stress, principally because of MacArthur.

In Europe, especially, there had been great fear that his management of the war would lead to a third – and probably cataclysmic – world war. However, many in the coalition also balked at the notion of maintaining Syngman Rhee's corrupt and unjust government in power. This was before even considering the cost of such a venture to a country like Britain, its economy still recovering from the Second World War.

For his part, General Ridgway sensed a shift in attitudes but a great deal depended on the attitude of the USSR. Kim Il-sung was determined not to let up on his army's operations, fearing that, when and if armistice negotiations began, he would be forced to make too many concessions. Mao Zedong had been very disappointed by the failure of the Fifth Offensive and, even though his country had already given so much to the conflict, he was in no mood to let this state of affairs continue.

Suddenly, all the talk was of a ceasefire. On 1 June 1951, UN Secretary-General, Trygve Lie, declared that the Security Council's objectives would have been achieved if a ceasefire was announced along the 38th Parallel. On 7 June, Secretary of State, Dean Acheson, speaking before a Senate committee, also said that United Nations forces would accept an armistice on the 38th Parallel. Then, on 23 June, the Soviet delegate to the United Nations, Yakov Malik, proposed a ceasefire in Korea.

Soviet personnel had been involved in advising Kim Il-sung's officers before and during the war and Soviet

116

air power had provided vital support for the Chinese and North Korean operations. Stalin, however, wanted Soviet involvement to remain indirect and he was not tempted into a more overt role even when Soviet territory was inadvertently attacked on a few occasions by US planes straying over the border. The Russians did not seek another world war. Stalin was convinced that one would eventually break out but he certainly did not want one at that particular point in time. To some extent, he was satisfied that his objectives had been fulfilled by the enmity that had been created between China and the United States. And anyway, the Democratic People's Republic of Korea had survived the war and it did not look as if the Americans would be able to do anything about it in the foreseeable future. The lack of desire for further action was evident in the reactions of right-wing US politicians to the war.

Stalin, meanwhile, had decided to explore diplomatic channels for ending the war. Both China and North Korea were so dependent on the Soviets that they could do little other than agree to his new approach. American efforts to this end were led by the diplomat George Kennan (1904-2005). Kennan had been the original advocate of a policy of containment of the USSR during the Cold War and his thinking also inspired the Truman Doctrine which sought to counter Soviet geopolitical expansion. Harry Truman had given a speech in March 1947, espousing this policy, and promising to help any nation threatened by communism. Having worked at the State Department in the 1930s and 1940s, Kennan had found it difficult to work under Acheson, and left the diplomatic service in 1950. He had been particularly critical of US policy in Korea, accusing the administration of a failure to identify its basic objectives on the peninsula early enough. But Kennan was an acknowledged expert on the Soviet Union and he had the requisite skills to undertake exceptionally delicate negotiations with the Russians, while, at the same time, not being employed by the US government.

He met a number of times with the Soviet UN delegate, Malik, a man he knew well. In a meeting in June, Malik confirmed that the Soviet Union was open to bringing the conflict in Korea to a conclusion and the *People's Daily* in Beijing endorsed the Soviet initiative. The change in Soviet policy towards the West was made public on 23 June when Malik, interviewed on the radio in New York, spoke of the Soviet desire to broker a better relationship with the West and expressed the hope that a ceasefire could be achieved in Korea. Truman immediately indicated that the United States would respond positively but only if the communists were genuine in their desire for peace.

These statements were welcomed by the United Nations. The British Foreign Secretary, Herbert Morrison, intimated to the British cabinet that they were promising but that everyone should exercise caution until the Soviets proved that they were serious. Naturally, there was not the same welcome for the peace moves from Syngman Rhee and Kim Il-sung. Rhee looked on horrified, feeling betrayed and believing that America was showing weakness. But, like Kim, there was nothing he could do about it.

Negotiations Begin

It was a different Korean War now. Whereas it had previously been a case of each side launching offensives and campaigns which were bloody and savage, it now became a war that was conducted less frenetically, although many of the engagements between the two forces remained bloody ones. The UN and communist delegations met for the first time on 10 July in Kaesong, a town just over the 38th Parallel in the west of North Korea. Little did they know the trials and tribulations that lay ahead in the next two years of negotiations.

In a message to Washington, Ridgway was in no doubt that the government should adopt a tough line in the talks:

'To sit down with these men and deal with them as representatives of an enlightened and civilised people is to deride one's own dignity and to invite the disaster their treachery will bring upon us.'

The UNC delegation was headed by US Navy Vice Admiral Turner Joy (1895-1956) while the communist group was led by the Russian-born North Korean General Nam Il (1915-76). It may, in retrospect, seem a pity that the talks were conducted by the military and not by diplomats. In addition, it soon became apparent that the two sides had differing agendas. The Chinese and North Koreans were seeking a major propaganda opportunity, acting as if they were actually receiving the surrender of the UNC and the arrival of the UNC delegation under a white flag was treated as if they were capitulating. The UNC group's seats were lower than the other side's and the language used by the communists was inflammatory – phrases such as 'the murderer Rhee' and 'your puppet on Formosa'. There were endless adjournments and debate about the most basic details. A request was made for the Red Cross to visit prisoners of war being held by the communists but it was denied. A nadir was reached on 10 August when the two sides spent two hours and eleven minutes staring across the table at each other in complete silence. Then, on 22 August, the communist delegation walked out of the negotiations, claiming that the United Nations Coalition had tried to kill the members of their delegation in an air attack.

For the Chinese, the time taken up by the five weeks of talks was very precious. It allowed them to reinforce with artillery, especially as the UNC next wanted to target the Hwachon Reservoir that supplied Seoul with both water and electricity. It was a bloody campaign with the aptly named Heartbreak Ridge and Bloody Ridge changing hands repeatedly between August and

October. Eventually, they ended up in American hands. And it was evident that things were not going well for the communists. To the west, UNC troops penetrated 19 miles north of the 38th Parallel. It was enough to persuade the communists to return to the negotiating table on 25 October 1951. This time, a neutral location was chosen – Panmunjom (now Panmunjeom) in the no-man's-land in North Hwanghae Province that separated the combatants.

Fresh orders went out to Van Fleet on 12 November. He was to restrict his troops' operations to defensive duties only on the current front which was now being called the Main Line of Resistance (MLR). It was permissible to stage local attacks, but any action involving a force greater than battalion strength had to be authorised by Ridgway himself. The reason for this became apparent when the UN delegation announced a negotiating proposal; if the communists signed an armistice within the next 30 days, the UNC would agree to make the existing front the border between the two countries. This, of course, was intended to be a carrot with which to lead the communists to a rapid conclusion to the conflict, but it also represented a signal to the communists that the UNC had no further territorial aspirations in Korea. The communists immediately ratified the proposal but then wasted the next 30 days talking about nothing. Of course, while the empty talk proceeded, their troops were establishing impressive and unassailable defensive positions, with trenches and tunnels dug into the hillsides along the 155-mile front from coast to coast. Their defences were 15 to 25 miles deep and they now had around 855,000 men facing the UNC. But these positions would, in fact, form the basis for the eventual armistice line that would be agreed some 19 months later.

The communists were very satisfied with their negotiating strategy. They were well aware that the people of the West were tired of Korea and they also knew that the UNC would never be prepared to accept the very high number of casualties that would result from any offensive aimed at breaking through their new defensive line. They were very happy, therefore, to play a long game in negotiations but also to launch an offensive every now and then to create UNC casualties and thereby keep up the pressure on the enemy.

The Talks

There was a general election in Britain in October 1951. By that time, the Labour government, led by Clement Attlee, was worn out. Several of its leading lights were ill or too old and the party, which enjoyed a majority of just five seats, was seriously divided, especially by the cost of rearmament. There had also been hard-fought major domestic reforms. They were defeated by Winston Churchill's Conservatives, and it would be 13 years before Labour was again in power. However, it was a result that was warmly welcomed by Washington. Truman and Acheson had a good relationship with the new prime minister but it would be sorely tested by the Korean War and Churchill's desire to secure a measure of détente with the Soviet Union in 1953.

Meanwhile, in Panmunjom the talks were being conducted in a febrile atmosphere. Each side looked upon the other with contempt and they were both guilty of issuing propaganda statements. But both sides were also acutely aware that victory was impossible for either of them, rendering them wary of making early or unnecessary concessions. They both wanted an end to the conflict but each of them was prepared to wait it out until the other side grew bored or tired.

The main issues being discussed at the talks were the demarcation line, the rebuilding of airfields and the fate of prisoners of war. On the matter of the demarcation line, the UNC proposal to maintain the existing one was greeted with dismay by the US Joint Chiefs. They were concerned that this was an early concession that would be perceived as a sign of weakness. Supervision was a problem but they felt that, if they threatened China with tough action, then they could obtain assurances on supervision. Sanctions were considered by the JCS – a naval blockade of China or the bombing of airbases in China and Manchuria. British military chiefs were of the opinion that such action would take too long to have any impact and that it could even prove dangerous. Acheson met with the new British Foreign Secretary, Anthony

Eden, in Rome at a meeting of foreign ministers in December 1951 to discuss Korea, and Eden indicated to him that his country would support the bombing of Chinese airbases in Manchuria if necessary, but could not agree to the bombing of towns and cities in China. Britain also believed that China was building up its air strength which would inevitably provide a greater threat to the troops on the ground. It was pointed out that it was in the interests of China and North Korea to prolong the negotiations for as long as possible.

Progress began to be made at Panmunjom, particularly with reference to the demarcation line and arrangements for inspections. The communists wanted the inspection teams to include Poland, Czechoslovakia and the Soviet Union but, of course, the inclusion of the Soviets was not something with which the UNC was going to agree. A conference was proposed, to be held within three months of the signing of an armistice and with the objective of devising a long-term solution to the future of the Korean peninsula.

The rebuilding of airfields was a thorny issue. The UNC wanted any agreement to include the codicil that there should be no extension of runways in order to ensure that jet aircraft could not land or take off. Finally, it was agreed to allow inspection of airfields by neutral bodies in December 1951. To Britain and the United States, who had expected more difficulty in having this accepted, it seemed a positive step.

The POW Question

Unexpectedly, however, the matter of POWs proved much more intractable. According to the Geneva Convention, agreed in 1949, those captured in war should be returned at the conclusion of hostilities to the states for which they fought. This appeared eminently sensible but it failed to deal with the unusual situation where a POW did not want to return to the country for which he or she fought. In the Korean War this was a real issue. Many of the troops who served in the armies of North Korea or China felt no particular loyalty to the nations under whose flag they fought. In fact, there were many in the Chinese army who had merely been transferred from Kuomintang (nationalist) armies to communist ones when they surrendered, were captured or when their commanders had switched sides, as happened often in the closing stages of the Chinese civil war. Efforts were made, of course, to convert these soldiers to communism, but many did not convert and so felt little loyalty to the communist system. Others were press-ganged into the North Korean army or had been in the ROK army and had been captured and forced to fight for North Korea. Therefore, it was very complicated.

The United States had signed the Geneva Convention but had not yet ratified it while the Chinese had not been involved in the creation of the convention as Chiang Kai-shek's Kuomintang regime had represented China. Aware that to allow voluntary repatriation could prove an embarrassment for them, the communists insisted that all POWs should be returned to the country they had been fighting for when captured. Truman, on the other hand, did not believe in coercing people, and had seen the desperate scenes when Russian prisoners of war were compulsorily sent back to the Soviet Union after the Second World War. As has been noted, his administration had also been severely criticised for failing to stand up to communism and a tough stance on the question of POWs gave him the opportunity to boost his anti-communist credentials.

Of course, there was also the question of UNC POWs being held by the communists. They were being treated badly, kept in harsh conditions and many were suffering from malnutrition and disease. Truman's tough stand was inevitably going to delay their release which would make the president very unpopular with the prisoners' families and friends. The British took the same stand, fully expecting that the standards of the Geneva Convention would be adhered to.

A large number of North Korean and Chinese POWs were held in camps in South Korea that were guarded by ROK and American troops although they were not given a very high priority. There were insufficient guards and little thought was given to the internal functioning of the camps. The prisoners began to form anti-communist or pro-communist hierarchies within the camps and there was a great deal of brutality. Prisoners were coerced by these groups into declaring whether they wanted to return to the states they had fought for, all depending on the loyalties of the camp leaders. At the same time, Kuomintang agents who were brought in as interpreters to camps in which the prisoners were Chinese, pressurised POWs into claiming that they did not want to return to China. In the same way, South Korean agents pressurised North Korean POWs in other camps. During 1952, there were riots in a number of camps, arising out of the poor conditions in which prisoners were being held. This gave a lie to the declarations of the US State Department and the British Foreign Office that the screening of POWs for return home or settlement in South Korea was running smoothly.

In May 1952, serious rioting erupted on the island of Koje-do (now Geojedo) in which the American camp commander was taken prisoner by the pro-communist rioters. Violence had been rising and the prisoners had protested about the conditions in the camp. Koje-do had become a propaganda vehicle for the communists and was also an ideological hotbed, a situation that the Americans failed to address. On 7 May, the camp commandant, Brigadier Francis Dodd (1899-1973), entered the camp's Compound 76, an area holding 6,400 of the most rabidly communist prisoners. At 3.15pm, as he was about to leave the compound, a whistle was blown and he was suddenly surrounded by prisoners and taken hostage. A sign was painted that read: 'WE CAPTURE DODD AS LONG AS OUR DEMAND WILL BE SOLVED HIS SAFETY IS SECURED, IF THERE

HAPPEN BRUTAL ACT SUCH AS SHOOTING, HIS LIFE IS IN DANGER.'

The camp was immediately surrounded by tanks and gunboats anchored off the island. On 9 May, General Van Fleet arrived to take command of the situation personally, by which time there were around 15,000 UNC troops on the island. The following night, Dodd was released unharmed, though it transpired that he had humiliatingly signed a document that seemed to justify the prisoners' case. In the coming days a stream of high-profile officials visited the island to berate the authorities there for their lack of control. But little changed and, in the following months, things went from bad to worse. In fact, between July 1951 and July 1952, no fewer than 115 prisoners died in rioting in the camps. The British responded positively to the United States' request that she provide troops for guarding the camps but the Canadians were not eager to comply, reluctant to be associated with the incident at Koje-do. They took days to agree. The Koje-do incident opened up the whole question of the treatment of Chinese and North Korean POWs. The British Foreign Secretary, Anthony Eden, was embarrassed when he was given misleading information that he shared in parliament. The United Nations was equally unhappy to discover the truth of the camps.

The matter of POWs was pushed temporarily to the sidelines by the sudden bombing of power stations on the Yalu River by American planes. The decision to do so was taken unilaterally by the United States and neither Britain nor the other members of the coalition were consulted or even informed about it. Making it more embarrassing was the fact that the British Defence Minister was in Washington when the raids took place and was completely in the dark about them. The US State Department eventually apologised for the oversight. Naturally, the bombing called into question just how serious the UNC was about the armistice negotiations and the talks would inevitably become much more difficult as a result. In Britain, the Labour Party moved a motion critical of the action, but Prime Minister Winston Churchill embarrassed the opposition by revealing that, while in power, the Attlee government had actually accepted the bombing because it believed it would represent a strong response to a new Chinese offensive.

In Britain, some in the Foreign Office were dubious about the strong line being followed over repatriation of Korean and Chinese POWs, but Prime Minister Churchill supported it, believing it wrong to return POWs forcibly to their homelands and abandon them to torture or death. It was believed early in 1952 that between 10 and 25 per cent of POWs would not want to be repatriated, that around 116,000 out of 132,000 would choose to go back and 18,000 out of 38,000 civilians. The screening process carried out in April 1952 found that about 70,000 wanted to go back to North Korea and China but, after more screening, that number rose to 82,000. Eventually 82,500 were repatriated and 50,000 decided to stay in South Korea.

By the summer of 1952 the talks had been going on for almost a year. Initially, there had been optimism that an armistice would be signed very soon and all parties could all move on. Now the fear was that, with things dragging on interminably, the war could flare up again at any moment and they would be right back where they started.

Other Voices

Within the United Nations, there were some figures trying to break the stalemate – the Indian Prime Minister, Jawaharlal Nehru (1889-1964), Lester Pearson (1897-1972), the Canadian Secretary of State for External Affairs and the British Foreign Secretary, Anthony Eden. Nehru had long been a very vocal critic of America while Pearson was concerned about the POW situation. Eden supported voluntary repatriation and thought that the Americans had handled the issue very badly. He believed the solution to the problem lay with the General Assembly if the ideas of the Indians were presented well and then followed up through diplomatic channels.

The Indian representative at the United Nations was the abrasive and unpredictable Krishna Menon (1896-1974), a close associate of Nehru. He was unpopular with Washington and the British found him difficult and obstinate. While sensing growing pressure on America from its allies and other nations at the UN who occupied a more neutral position, Dean Acheson failed to impress. He had other matters to deal with, particularly the November 1952 US presidential election which was unlikely to deal kindly with the Democrats. Menon submitted the Indian proposal which the British regarded as not conclusive enough and lacking in detail. It advocated the establishment of a repatriation commission that would use nationality and domicile to classify POWs who would be given the right to put their case to the commission's members. The British, meanwhile, were considering a plan involving the disavowal of coercion by each side. They also recommended that nations neutral in the war should be brought in to ensure that the established procedures were followed correctly. Acheson was worried, however, that Britain, India and Canada were prepared to go too far in accommodating the wishes of the communists which would inevitably make the Truman administration appear weak. And, anyway, Washington had already agreed its approach to the problem earlier in 1952 and Acheson was uneasy about reopening the debate, particularly as he thought that what they had decided was the correct path to follow. The Indian proposal was worked on by the British, Indian and Canadian representatives but, although Anthony Eden felt sure the Americans would accept it, he was to be disappointed. Acheson still felt that the proposal was ambiguous and feared it would give the communists the opportunity to argue that the West was not fulfilling its obligations.

Lester Pearson, who was at the time President of the General Assembly, and Eden's deputy, Selwyn Lloyd (1904-78), tried and failed to arrive at a compromise with Acheson. Lloyd further urged compromise at a meeting of 21 states convened by the US Secretary of State on 17 November but again Acheson disagreed, enjoying the support of several other nations. Indeed, Acheson even began to urge Britain to move more towards the position that had been taken up by the United States. Eden was extremely frustrated and blamed Acheson for the stalemate, describing him as 'rigid, legalistic and difficult'. Meanwhile, both the British and American negotiating teams were leaking information to the press, undermining the other's position and blaming each other for the lack of a solution.

The situation was resolved by the Soviet Minister of Foreign Affairs, Andrei Vyshinsky (1883-1954). He launched a scathing attack on the Indian proposal during a speech in the First Committee of the General Assembly, one of the main UN committees, dealing with disarmament and international security. Most people were surprised by this because the Soviets would have been expected to have been pleased that the Indians had come up with a solution that was at variance to the position of the United States. Acheson adroitly, and opportunistically, leapt to the defence of the Indian proposition and said that, with a few changes, America would be able to support it. The proposal was carried in the General Assembly, the USSR and several of its allies voting against it.

Thus, the tension in the United Nations and between the United States and other members of the UNC was laid bare for all to see. And once again, it was evident that, even at times when it would have suited their objectives to do otherwise, the communists could be absolutely immovable. This had also been evident in January 1951 when China remained intransigent during discussions with the UN Secretary-General in New York.

Eisenhower Wins the Presidential Election

It had been 20 years since a Republican had occupied the Oval Office, but Dwight D Eisenhower won a landslide victory over Adlai Stevenson (1900-65) in November 1952, following an unpleasant election campaign dominated by the anti-communist crusade led by Senator Joseph McCarthy (1908-57). Eisenhower was an American Army general who had been Supreme Commander of the Allied Expeditionary Force in Europe during the Second World War and, most recently, he had been commander of NATO forces in Europe. A moderate conservative, the new president was a believer in the United States' global role. Naturally, his army career made him expert in defence issues but he was a political neophyte and there were some doubts about his skills in that arena. This was especially important in view of the growing power and influence of the right wing of his party, the Republicans.

Of concern to many were the appointments he would make to the great offices of state. Anthony Eden, for instance, was hopeful that John Foster Dulles (1888-1959) would not be appointed Secretary of State. Dulles also believed that America should fulfil its global responsibilities but was distrustful of Britain. Dulles had already stated his support for President Truman's stance on Korea, describing it as 'courageous, righteous, and in the national interest'. But he was also of the belief that Truman had allowed the Soviets more freedom to confront the USA than it should have. He was a believer in retaliation using nuclear weapons and hoped to inhibit Russia's actions around the world with that threat. This led him to the opinion that America should not become preoccupied by local wars fought in distant lands against regimes supported by the Russians and, consequently, he believed that the United States should withdraw from its involvement in Korea.

But, for Eisenhower, Dulles could prove very useful. He had already demonstrated his considerable diplomatic skills while negotiating the peace treaty with Japan in 1950-51 and, significantly, he was able to work with the left and right wings of the Republican Party in Congress. Therefore, to the chagrin of Eden and Churchill, he was appointed to the post. Meanwhile, Eisenhower took a stance regarding POWs that was contrary to the previous

US position as championed by Dean Acheson, and gave his approval to the Indian proposal.

In 1952, there were rumours, spread by the communists, that the UNC was using bacteriological warfare on the Korean peninsula. It was a desperate effort to persuade POWs that capitalism was ruthless and to influence public opinion in the West. In the winter of 1950-51, the North Koreans had already accused the United States of spreading typhus but this grew into an accusation of a more widespread use of such methods. Russian, Chinese and North Korean media ran stories suggesting the Americans had used anthrax, cholera and bubonic plague. To investigate the veracity of such accusations, an international scientific commission was created. The evidence its members examined was mostly provided by Korean peasants who told them of odd incidents and infected flies that had appeared following the flight of American planes overhead. Nonetheless, no proof was found that these claims were true.

Prisoner of War Conditions

The success of the Chinese offensive at the outset of their involvement in the war had resulted in the capture of considerable numbers of American troops and some British, and these prisoners were held in conditions that were often harsh and brutal. As well as the constant threat of violence, the quality and amount of food and drink provided was poor and they were often subjected to vicious forced marches. All of this as the weather worsened and the temperatures plummeted.

The majority of POWs were in the hands of the Chinese, captured following the Chinese intervention in the conflict. These prisoners were treated a little better than those in North Korean hands. The fact remained, however, that neither North Korea nor the People's Republic of China were signatories to the Geneva Convention which stipulated how prisoners of war should be treated. The North Koreans, in particular, sought to manipulate the prisoners psychologically, lowering their morale while also making efforts to convince them of the innate superiority of communism to capitalism. Strenuous efforts were made – especially by the North Koreans – to indoctrinate the prisoners of war and thereby convert them to the communist cause.

The British POW, General Sir Anthony Farrar-Hockley (1924-2006), was imprisoned at a camp on the Yalu. He wrote about the comportment expected of captives:

'After capture, prisoners must be friends and no longer adopt a hostile attitude; they must learn repentance and the meaning of peace. They are lucky to be alive after fighting for the capitalists and they should be grateful that they are prisoners of the Chinese and have the chance to study until they go home. The Lenient Policy is unchangeable but there must be no sabotage of study. A hostile attitude to study or any attempt to spoil other students' study will be punished. If you are friendly to us you will be treated as a friend, but the Lenient Policy has its limitations as regards our enemies.'

It goes without saying that those prisoners who did not behave accordingly were subjected to torture and horrific brutality but, even without that, life was cheap. By mid-1951, more than 50 per cent of American captives had died, most of these while under the control of the North Koreans. But from the end of that year, United Nations Coalition POWs were being held in camps run by the Chinese that were better organised and where the prisoners were treated less brutally.

Days in the camps were filled with meetings where the writings of Marx, Lenin and Chairman Mao were discussed and the advantages of communism over capitalism were constantly rammed home. Naturally, it was very boring to the UNC troops who generally did not respond well to the extracts from the works of the great communist philosophers with which they were presented. Indeed, they mimicked their captors' efforts at indoctrination relentlessly in the entertainments they staged in the camps, their guards ignorant of the jibes because their knowledge of English was non-existent. In further efforts to win the POWs over to the communist side, there were also visits from British communists or communist sympathisers. When the talks finally began in July 1951, conditions for UNC prisoners of war greatly improved since, with a possible armistice imminent, it was not desirable to have a high casualty rate amongst them.

There is little doubt that the treatment of POWs was bad on both sides. The UNC was mistaken in its approach, failing to manage and properly supervise its camps. It was also a mistake to introduce Kuomintang agents into the camps as they put undue pressure on the Chinese POWs to renounce communism. The Chinese and North Koreans indulged in horrific brutality in the first winter of the conflict and, of course, conditions in the camps were a disgrace. There is little doubt that things improved on both sides as time went on and the armistice approached. The actual logistics of getting POWs home or, at least, to where they wanted to be, would to a large extent depend on the attitude of the Soviets and the approach adopted by the new administration in Washington.

9

Moving Towards a Conclusion

Eisenhower Goes to Korea

In August 1951, Eisenhower had claimed that it had been a mistake to withdraw US troops from the Korean peninsula in 1949 as there were 'menacing signs from the north'. What he neglected to say was that he had actually been one of the Joint Chiefs of Staff who had passed the advice to the Truman administration that Korea was of little strategic interest to the United States and it would, therefore, be pointless to keep troops there. Truman and the Democratic Party were appalled by this and demanded to know what he would do about Korea if elected. Eventually, the response came from the Republican nominee that, were he to be elected, he would travel to Korea to assess the situation personally. The notion was presented in a simple, short phrase to be used by Eisenhower on the campaign trail – 'I shall go to Korea'. He was unsure about the idea and about the speech in which he would make the announcement, but he delivered it nationwide via television in Detroit on 24 October. At the end of the speech, he said he would make it his first priority, if elected, to bring an end to the conflict in Korea:

'That job requires a personal trip to Korea. I shall make that trip. Only in that way could I learn best how to serve the American people in the cause of peace. I shall go to Korea.'

He spent three days in Korea, visiting a Mobile Army Surgical Hospital, talking to wounded soldiers and meeting with Syngman Rhee who remained suspicious of the new president. He spent time with Generals Mark Clark (1896-1984) and Van Fleet and said at a press conference that he thought it unlikely that there was going to be 'a positive and decisive victory without possibly running the grave risk of enlarging the war'. He added, however: 'America will see it through.'

Generals Van Fleet and Clark had been expecting lengthy discussions about what the military options were for the continued execution of the war. What they got was Eisenhower discussing the best ways to persuade the communists to accept a ceasefire.

The first thing that Eisenhower did, in order to accomplish his objective of a truce, was to increase the size of the ROK army to 655,000, beginning in the spring of 1953. This would cost the United States

$1 billion per annum. The aim was, of course, to shift the burden of prosecuting the war onto South Korea. It was still evident that ROK troops were no match for the Chinese, but, fortunately, the newly-bolstered ROK force would not have to undergo a stringent military test against the enemy.

The test detonation by the USA of the first nuclear device that was of a size that made it practical for use by artillery was also significant for the negotiations. The Joint Chiefs were impressed and bellicose, as can be seen in a study that was published on 27 March 1953:

'The efficacy of atomic weapons in achieving greater results at less cost of effort in furtherance of US objectives in connection with Korea points to the desirability of re-evaluating the policy which now restricts the use of atomic weapons in the Far East… In view of the extensive implications of developing an effective conventional capability in the Far East, the timely use of atomic weapons should be considered against military targets affecting operations in Korea, and operationally planned as an adjunct to any possible military course of action involving direct action against Communist China and Manchuria.'

Then, on 19 May, the Joint Chiefs proposed air and naval attacks on China and Manchuria. These surprise attacks would include the employment of nuclear weapons. The proposal was supported by the National

Security Council. Meanwhile, John Foster Dulles was in India and he passed a message to Prime Minister Nehru that he should let Chinese Prime Minister Zhou Enlai know that if there was not sufficient progress in the negotiations, the United States would start to bomb north of the Yalu River. At the same time, Eisenhower announced that the US Navy would no longer be acting as a buffer between the Chinese mainland and Formosa. This led to a series of raids on the mainland by nationalists.

It is impossible to say to what extent many of these announcements were bluffs and whether the Americans would actually have used nuclear weapons but there is no doubt that the Soviets were wary of the belligerent new Secretary of State. Dulles bolstered this fear by stating at a National Security Council meeting in February that the United States had to make the idea of the use of nuclear weapons more acceptable. The Soviets, he said, had successfully managed to make atomic weapons somehow different to all other weapons, to have them put into a 'special' category. He was of the opinion that this distinction should be removed. Eisenhower was of the same opinion, believing that victory in Korea would be worth the cost. He suggested that the best place for a nuclear attack would be Kaesong in North Korea.

Would Eisenhower have gone ahead with such a strategy if nothing had changed? One likes to think that he would have resorted to such a risky act only if the Chinese had provoked him to do so. To employ nuclear weapons in the prevailing situation, a stalemate, would only have caused outrage around the world, especially amongst America's allies in the United Nations Coalition. It seems unlikely that it would have come to such a risky move, especially given the conservative nature of the president and the caution he invariably exercised.

It worked, however. It seems that the powers-that-be in the Soviet Union and China agreed that the new administration in Washington was now willing to introduce nuclear weapons to the Korean battlefield if things did not change around the negotiating table in Panmunjon and the United States was not allowed to make an honourable exit from the Korean peninsula.

The talks finally began to make progress.

The Bargaining Chips

It had become apparent early in the Korean War that it was unlikely it would be settled on terms which assured that the peninsula would be reunified. In fact, the terms and the negotiations always returned to the same sticking point – the prisoners. The prisoners were now the bargaining chips used by each side, as if they were hostages in a bank robbery.

The Red Cross had tried to achieve something for the prisoners in December 1952 when they had made efforts to arrange an exchange of sick and wounded POWs. 'A gesture for peace', they called it. General Clark was open to the idea but it was summarily rejected by China and the Soviet Union. Then, out of the blue, on 28 March 1953, the communists announced that they would, indeed, accept the exchange. Astonishingly, they added to their announcement that they hoped this would open the door to an agreement on the POW issue and, indeed, a ceasefire 'for which people throughout the world are longing'. Nonetheless, although Zhou Enlai confirmed Chinese acceptance of the exchange in a radio broadcast a couple of days later, he reiterated that China would not tolerate any exchange that left a single North Korean or Chinese soldier in UNC hands. In fact, he insisted that POWs who were in any doubt about returning to the country for which they fought, should be handed over to a neutral state which could carry out a proper independent investigation into each individual case. The Russians agreed to this process and offered their support in making it happen.

Despite initial American suspicion of China's proposal – it would not be the first time that an apparently simple notion was found to be fraught with complications in the armistice talks – they actually reached an agreement with the communists on 11 April. In what was termed Operation Little Switch, 700 Chinese troops and 5,100 North Koreans were to be sent back north while 450 South Korean and 150 non-South Korean POWs were to be dispatched in the other direction. The exchange took place between 20 April and 3 May at Panmunjom.

There was general revulsion at the condition of the

UNC POWs who were part of the exchange. It transpired that they had been subject to starvation, and their wounds and injuries had been left untreated for months. Many were also in a poor psychological condition. Nonetheless, negotiations reopened for another exchange. On 26 April, the full Western and communist delegations convened at Panmunjom for the first time in almost six months, in an attempt to select a neutral nation to which prisoners refusing to be repatriated could be sent. Switzerland was the suggestion of the United Nations, with the stipulation that no man should be held for more than two months. The communists countered with a period of six months and rejected Switzerland. Instead, after suggesting Pakistan, they changed tack completely, proposing a period of four months and a Neutral Nations Repatriation Commission that would be made up of Poland, Switzerland, Czechoslovakia, Sweden and India.

It was evident now that the communists were serious in their search for a conclusion to the war, encouraged, no doubt, by the new people holding the reins in Moscow. (Stalin had died on 5 March 1953). America was eager to press home its advantage and felt that the UNC force now held a strong position. General Mark Clark was given authority by Washington to intensify the bombing campaign, and North Korean dams were attacked in order to destroy crops and impede the supply of food. At that moment, the United Nations delegation at the talks presented what it described as a final proposal. One neutral power – not a commission – would screen all the POWs who were unwilling to go back to where they came from in Korea within 90 days. Were this not to happen, they added, all the North Korean prisoners in this category would be set free in South Korea in a month's time, plus they would increase the bombing of targets in North Korea.

Syngman Rhee and the Armistice Talks

Relations between Britain and the United States were at a low point in the spring and summer of 1953. There were issues over policies towards the communist states. Eisenhower and Churchill had different opinions on how to proceed. Stalin was dead and there could perhaps be an opportunity for improved East–West relations. Experts counselled caution. Churchill, however, was able to operate freely in the arena of foreign affairs due to the prolonged absence through illness from the Foreign Office of Anthony Eden. Britain's great war leader believed that there was a danger of the world slipping into global conflict and that the only way to avoid this was to reduce the tension by pursuing détente with the Soviet Union. He saw the Korean War and its conclusion as one way to do this, and wished to cooperate with the Russians to bring the war to a conclusion that was satisfactory for all. Eisenhower was not of the same opinion.

Churchill had been concerned, when he was returned as prime minister in 1951, that Eisenhower might make unsatisfactory concessions just to bring the war to an end. From the autumn of 1952, he became ever more critical of American policy in Korea, probably influenced by the arguments over the Indian proposal to deal with the thorny POW issue. He was horrified by the American determination to issue what was called a 'greater sanctions statement' after the armistice was signed, a statement that was to serve as a blunt warning to China about what would happen if the terms of the armistice were not adhered to. This was too much stick and not nearly enough carrot for Churchill as he sought to create a much more harmonious atmosphere amongst the world's great powers.

But there was little or no agreement with Churchill, even in his own cabinet. And Eisenhower and Dulles thought his approach unwise. They wanted to wait to see how the new leaders in Moscow were going to act. Churchill, however, was not for waiting and he contacted Vyacheslav Molotov (1890-1986), the Soviet foreign minister, directly, telling him that it was time tension between East and West was reduced and hoping that the end of the Korean War would contribute to that. Molotov's response was positive, reassuring the British prime minister that all had been prepared for a successful conclusion to the talks. All that stood in the way was the pig-headed president of South Korea.

While the negotiations went on and the entire world awaited an end to hostilities in Korea, Syngman Rhee and his supporters were in despair, watching all their hopes disappear. Rhee was now well aware that Eisenhower would be very happy to accept a ceasefire based upon the status quo and, with that, the implication that Korea would be permanently divided. Such an agreement would also condemn the Republic of Korea to constant threat from its northern rival. He railed against it, declaring emphatically that he would never accept a settlement that did not remove the Chinese from North Korea and, therefore, remove the threat of attack, effectively a demilitarisation of the north.

His warnings did not fall on deaf ears in South Korea and even his opponents became concerned about what was seen as a betrayal by their allies, the Americans. There were anti-American rallies in South Korea's cities, perhaps organised by agents of the president, but expressing genuine fears about what would happen to their country. With the Americans gone, what was to stop the communists from once again flooding over the 38th Parallel? In the National Assembly, Rhee's protestations were joined by the opposition.

In desperation, Rhee wrote to Eisenhower that, if a ceasefire agreement was reached at Panmunjom that permitted the Chinese to maintain their forces in North Korea, then the army of the Republic of Korea would continue to fight, even without American and United Nations support, and would stop only when the Chinese had been forced back over the Yalu River into their own territory. It was, of course, a fairly ridiculous statement, given the inadequate performance of the ROK army thus far in the conflict. His threat was disturbing, however, because there was a danger that he could derail the armistice negotiations. General Clark therefore made strenuous efforts to persuade the South Korean president that his fears were groundless, that America would continue to support the enlargement of the ROK army, no matter what emerged from the armistice talks. Clark was convinced that he had succeeded in pacifying the irascible president, cabling the Joint Chiefs: 'He is bargaining now to get a security pact, to obtain more economic aid, and to make his people feel he is having a voice in the armistice negotiations.' But, as ever, the stubborn Rhee would have a lot more to say on the matter.

The Chinese put forward another proposal on 26 April. Three months after an armistice, prisoners who rejected repatriation would be moved to a neutral state for six months. There they would be evaluated by representatives of the government of their original state. At the end of this process, they would remain incarcerated while their fate was decided. When the UN rejected the proposal, relations between the two sides degenerated into recriminations being shouted across the table by both sides. The mood returned to what it had been at the start of the negotiations. Eventually, when it became obvious that no further progress was going to be made, the talks were adjourned.

It was at this point that Washington gave in, making the concession that it had refused to make for so long. To the embarrassment of Mark Clark and the ire of

Syngman Rhee, it was decided to hand over to the neutral Indian supervisory commission Koreans as well as Chinese who did not want to be repatriated. The furious Rhee threatened to remove the ROK army from the authority of the United Nations Coalition and the Americans. In the background, however, the Americans prepared to implement Plan Ever-Ready which would see control of the Republic of Korea seized from Rhee and his administration. Rhee would be informed that, if he failed to accept the terms of the armistice agreed at Panmunjom, he would be held incommunicado in protective custody. A replacement, in the person of the prime minister, Chang Taek-sang (1893-1969), would be installed or, if he turned down the position, a military government would be formed.

On 25 May, when it looked certain that the Americans' proposal was going to be acceptable to the other side, Mark Clark informed Syngman Rhee. Rhee was, naturally, bitterly disappointed and was scathing about the armistice proposals, seeing them as merely appeasement of the communists by the United Nations. Meanwhile, the talks went on and eventually, on 8 June, the two sides reached agreement on the repatriation of POWs. It was agreed that any prisoner who wanted to go home would be allowed to do so at once. Those prisoners who were reluctant to return to their home country would remain with the Repatriation Commission for a period of 90 days. During this time, their government would be able to meet with them at any time. A 'political conference' would then assess their fate for a further 30 days and, following that, any who remained would be deemed to be civilians and would be permitted to stay in whichever country they found themselves in at the time.

The Americans were horrified, however, when, on 18 June 1953, the South Koreans threw open the gates of four of the camps where enemy POWs were being held and allowed them to walk free; 25,000 North Koreans who had not wanted to return to their native land disappeared into the countryside. The gates were almost certainly thrown open on the orders of Syngman Rhee. The fugitives were helped by ROK soldiers and police, given blankets and directed towards shelter, while South Korean radio warned them to be careful because American troops were hunting them down. US troops were rushed in to guard the compounds but the action continued and, within a few days, there were only around 9,000 of the original 35,400 North Korean troops still in captivity. Of those who escaped, the Americans succeeded in recapturing only around 1,000.

Rhee's action was especially galling to the Americans due to the danger of the communists abandoning the armistice talks. They did walk out for two-and-a-half weeks but returned on 8 July. Washington, of course, denounced the South Korean action, distancing itself from it. However, the Chinese may have been secretly pleased that the prisoners had been released. It freed them from the embarrassment of being rejected by their former citizens.

The Fighting Escalates

All that stood in the way of an armistice was President Rhee. His public agreement with the armistice plan had to be obtained but he was proving to be obdurate. The Americans reiterated their threats that, if he did not give his consent, they would abandon his regime. Of course, they could not afford for any news of these threats to be conveyed to the communists whose bargaining hand would be made immeasurably stronger with such information. General Clark and Eisenhower's special envoy, Walter Robinson, engaged in talks with Rhee that dragged on for two months, through June and July.

Around this time, while the talks continued, there was some of the heaviest fighting of the war, the communists eager to demonstrate just how superior their forces were to those of the ROK. One hundred thousand attacked five divisions of South Korean troops, driving them back five miles before United Nations artillery entered the fray, firing a massive 2.7 million rounds in the month of June alone. This was one million more rounds fired than in any month of the war to date.

Knowing the end was approaching, the communists naturally tried to achieve the most favourable position that they could, launching attacks both in the air and on the ground. There had been a massive aircraft building programme in Manchuria during the winter and UNC intelligence officers had become very concerned by this. Large numbers of MiG-15s had been constructed

152

but what was more worrying was the appearance of jet bombers – the Ilyushin Il-28 which was a medium-range aircraft and posed a grave threat for South Korea. Thus, the last few months of the war saw American Air Force Sabres and Navy Panthers in the air seeking out the enemy's new planes. In June 1953, this resulted in the highest number of downed communist planes of the war – 74 MiGs were destroyed. Many of the young US pilots, gaining combat experience early in their careers, would go on to command squadrons later, in the Vietnam War.

Meanwhile, American Air Force bombers – both Boeing B-29 Superfortresses and fighter bombers – continued to pound North Korea. And new names took to the sky such as the all-weather night-fighters, the Douglas F3D Skyknight and the Lockheed F-94 Starfire, providing protection for the aging B-29s. Despite the Chinese build-up of aircraft, the Americans remained dominant in the air as they had been since the start of the war.

On the ground, the communists were desperate to go out on a winning note. There was a dangerous balance, of course. They had to do just enough to be able to call it a victory, but not so much that the UNC would retaliate massively. There was also the danger, of course, of the UN walking away from the negotiating table. In March, they engaged along the front in small actions but the following month was wet and everything slowed down again in the resultant mud. In late May and early June, as the negotiations reached their final stages, they once more resorted to probing the UNC line. There was a major attack when agreement on POWs was reached on 8 June, an attempt to improve their position at the very last minute. They struck the middle of the Eighth Army line, on rough terrain, and a series of pushes was also launched against the right flank of US IX Corps and across the ROK II Corps front. For about ten days they attacked, trying to push back the troops who were occupying a bulge in the line that stretched from near Kumhwa towards Mundung-ni. They succeeded in driving the South Koreans back a few miles in some places, incurring heavy casualties as they did so, but the attacks faded away. It might have been that they were merely testing the ROK army or even sending a message to Syngman Rhee. They also now well and truly had the initiative. Following the liberation of the POWs, it was clear that the Americans had failed to control their client, Rhee. The communists milked this for all it was worth, demanding numerous recesses in the talks as Lieutenant General William K Harrison (1895-1987) found himself covering the same old ground.

On the night of 13 July, the Chinese launched their biggest ground initiative since 1951 when six Chinese battalions, numbering around 80,000 troops, attacked the ROK II line in central Korea. As ever, they suffered exceptionally heavy casualties but, after three days of fierce fighting, they had forced the ROK troops back some six miles. The UNC line had been pierced in two places and two divisions were in danger of being cut off. Retreating back to the Kumsong River, the South Koreans struggled to hang on to even that position. At that point Clark brought forward US troops, including the 187th Airborne Regiment that had been flown in from Japan. The ROK troops regrouped to launch a counter-attack but, failing to retake all the territory they had lost, dug into ridges that looked down on the valley of the Kumsong. Meanwhile, along the front there were small actions, including some fierce fighting for hills that had been designated to be within the Demilitarised Zone. Once again, the amount of ordnance employed by the Americans was prodigious and the number of men lost by the communists was staggering. This was not just an exercise in being able to claim a victory in the last days of the war. It was also a message from the communists to the Americans and the UNC that they were ready and able to continue fighting.

The Signing of the Armistice

Promised American aid and deals for the foreseeable future, Rhee finally caved in on 9 July, although he declared, with his customary obstinacy, that he would not sign the armistice. He added, however, that he would not stand in the way of the agreement. Meanwhile, the United Nations had made it clear to Rhee that they would not tolerate or support any independent military action undertaken by ROK troops. Three days later, on

12 July, the United States and the Democratic People's Republic of Korea made a joint announcement that they had agreed on terms for an end to hostilities on the Korean peninsula.

When it came to the actual signing of the armistice there were, inevitably, logistical problems. Liaison officers had worked out all the details such as where the Demilitarised Zone would be situated, but even the question of who would do the actual signing and who would act as witnesses were problematical. It was all about the manipulation of the situation to gain an advantage and to make one side appear a winner compared to the other. A copy of Pablo Picasso's famous illustration *Dove of Peace* was hung inside the building, but the Americans objected to it and had it covered up because Picasso was a communist.

The building where the signing was to take place was built overnight in Panmunjom and completed early on the morning of 27 July. When Mark Clark arrived, he insisted on a new entrance being built so that the UN delegation would not have to enter the building through the communist area. At the UN southern entrance, there was a guard of honour, made up of members of each of the armies that had fought in the war, although the Republic of Korea army was notable by its absence. Rhee had forbidden his men to participate in an event with which he so strongly disagreed.

The ceremony, which ultimately proved to be something of an anticlimax, began at exactly 10am on 27 July, when the two delegations entered the building from the north and south. Press and spectators had filed into the conference hall half an hour earlier. The delegations knew each other well by this time because they had been talking for 2 years and 17 days and it has been estimated that they had been involved in some 575 meetings during that time. The United Nations party, dressed in plain khakis, was led by Lieutenant General Harrison who sat down at a table on which was positioned a small United Nations flag and began to sign each of the nine blue-covered copies of the armistice agreement. The agreement stated in its preamble:

'The undersigned... in the interest of stopping the Korean Conflict, with its great toll of suffering and bloodshed on both sides, and with the objective of establishing an armistice which will ensure a complete cessation of hostilities and of all acts of armed force in Korea until a final settlement is achieved, do individually, collectively, and mutually agree to accept and to be bound and governed by the conditions and terms of armistice set forth in the following Articles and Paragraphs.'

Aides exchanged the signed copies and they were signed by the other side. The signatory for the communists, who were wearing full, formal uniform, was General Nam Il who sat at a table on which there was a small North Korean flag. Not a word was exchanged between the two parties and there were not even any handshakes.

The two men sat signing for 12 minutes while in the distance could be heard the sound of artillery fire. It would continue for another 12 hours until the armistice formally took effect. Without exchanging a single word, they stood up and looked coldly at one another before turning and leaving the way they had come in. It had been an extraordinary few minutes.

Twelve hours later, silence finally returned to the hills, lakes and valleys of Korea and the war was over. Harrison later wrote of the experience, declaring that it 'capped my career, but it was a cap without a feather'.

Interestingly, Harrison had the dubious honour of being the first American commander in history to have signed an armistice without breathing the scent of victory, a fact that he regretted deeply. It was his own personal opinion that the UN should have prosecuted the war to the Yalu River, bombing beyond it into Chinese territory. Like most of his colleagues, he believed the only way to end a war was with victory on the battlefield.

It is worth remembering that South Korea never did sign the armistice agreement, due to Syngman Rhee's antipathy towards it and his refusal to accept the division of Korea. It is also worthy of note that it established only a cessation of hostilities and not a normalisation of relations between the South and the North. Neither was it a peace treaty, and no formal peace treaty bringing the war to an end has ever been signed by the main players in the war. Importantly, a Military Demarcation Line (MDL) was created and a Demilitarised Zone which was agreed to be a 2.5-mile area between the two countries. It follows the Kansas Line which is where the front line was at the moment the armistice was signed. In recent years this has become the most heavily defended border in the world. It is not much different from what the border was at the start of the conflict in June 1950.

Arrangements were also made for ensuring stability in the region so that a political conference could be staged to arrive at a full settlement. A Military Armistice Commission was created that would meet at Panmunjom and the Neutral Nations Supervisory Commission was established.

The Prisoner Exchange

The armistice agreement stated that:

> 'Within sixty (60) days after this agreement becomes effective each side shall, without offering any hindrance, directly repatriate and hand over in groups all those prisoners of war in its custody who insist on repatriation to the side to which they belonged at the time of capture.'

The exchange of prisoners eventually started on 5 August. It was supervised by the Neutral Nations Repatriation Commission consisting, as noted before, of Switzerland, Poland, Czechoslovakia, Sweden and India.

India chaired the commission and also provided the troops to manage the exchange, a specially created unit known as Custodial Force India which proved worthy of its British military training. As was often the case with this difficult and frustrating conflict, however, the exchange inevitably ran into problems. The 22,604 non-repatriates – those who did not wish to go home – were about a third North Korean and two-thirds Chinese. These men had been through a seemingly endless process of screening, evaluation and classification. They had not been made 'civilian detainees' and neither had they been released when Rhee had ordered the prison gates to be thrown open. The communists had proposed that they wished to question or, as they put it, 'explain' their situation and they were sure they would then want to go back home. These 'explanations' involved the prisoner being brought into a tent where a team of communists would shout at him for several hours. This haranguing failed to work, however, and even after it most prisoners still rejected the notion of returning where they came from. Eventually, as the 'explanations' became increasingly angry and threatening, the Indian supervisory force would have to intervene. It was a process that continued in this manner until January 1954 when the Indians, revolted by what was going on, unilaterally declared that it was time to end it. In total, a mere 628 of more than 22,000 opted to return to their place of origin. Those who were left were free to begin a new life in South Korea, although most chose to settle in Nationalist China.

In all, 12,757 captives were returned by the communists of whom 7,848 were of South Korean origin, 1,312 were United Nations personnel and the remainder, 3,597, were American. Of the twenty-one Americans and one Briton who chose to remain in North Korea, a number drifted back to the United States, disillusioned with life in a communist country. The British defector was Andrew Condron, of 41 Royal Marine Commando, who was influenced to live in China by reports of the use of biological warfare, although he is said by friends to have also been motivated by an interest in Marxism and Maoism. Condron eventually returned to Britain in 1962, disillusioned by increasing Chinese xenophobia, but claiming to have no regrets.

The UN handed over 75,823 prisoners, of whom 70,000 were North Korean and the remainder Chinese. These captives were deliriously happy to be going home but they were eager to make it look as if they had suffered bad treatment in the hands of the West. Some had already ripped their clothing to make it appear that they were in rags and from the backs of the trucks that were taking them home, they threw away all the luxuries they had been given, such as toothpaste and cigarettes. Many took off their clothing and boots and threw them away too, freeing themselves of anything that was associated with the hated capitalism and unperturbed by returning home naked.

UNC prisoners who had been held captive in North Korea presented a different spectacle altogether. Many were very thin through deprivation and many were also mentally scarred. There were those suffering the terrible guilt of having collaborated with the enemy just to stay alive. They were greeted beneath a 'Welcome Home' arch by a huge team of people – doctors, psychiatrists and interrogators. It would be unbearably difficult for many of these men to readjust to normal life again.

'The Century's Nastiest Little War'

The ceasefire came into effect at 10pm on 27 July, but in the few hours before that, artillery fire was doubled on some sections of the front, an exercise in futility if ever there was one. Many found it hard to believe that it would stop at the allotted time, but on the stroke of 10, silence suddenly enveloped each side's position. A message was passed to British troops in one sector that they could, if they wished, go out into no-man's-land, although officers were forbidden from doing so. They were greeted by groups of Chinese soldiers offering them beer and rice wine and little glass rings on which was inscribed the word 'Peace'. The UN troops offered chocolate and cigarettes. This happened all along the front.

But the fact that no one had won pervaded the atmosphere on both sides of the line. In all of their history, it was the first time it had happened to the Americans and many of the troops questioned what it had, ultimately, all been about. The conflict was described by military historian, Brigadier General SLA Marshall (1900-77), as 'the century's nastiest little war', although that description might more appropriately be given either to the Vietnam War a decade later or to several other twentieth-century conflicts. In all, 1,319,000 Americans served in Korea, of whom 33,629 lost their lives and 105,785 were wounded. A staggering 45 per cent of all American casualties were incurred after the start of armistice negotiations. A total of 415,000 ROK army soldiers were killed and 429,000 were wounded. Britain, Canada, New Zealand and Australia lost 1,263 men and 4,817 were wounded; 1,800 soldiers from other nations participating on the UNC side – Belgium, Colombia, Ethiopia, France, Greece, the Netherlands, Luxemburg, the Philippines, Thailand and Turkey – were lost and 7,000 were wounded. It is hard to know exactly how many North Korean and Chinese casualties there actually were but it is estimated that anywhere between 398,000 and 589,000 died with more than 145,000 missing. Almost 700,000 were wounded.

In terms of civilians, again it is difficult to be exact, but it is estimated that between 2 and 3 million lost their lives in the conflict. Of these, in South Korea, 373,599 people were killed and 229,625 were wounded. In addition, 387,744 South Korean civilians were missing or perhaps had been abducted. In North Korea, it is estimated that around 1,550,000 civilians had been killed or wounded.

The war saw many atrocities and massacres of civilians.

They were perpetrated by both sides but most seem to have been committed by the South Koreans. At the very start of the conflict, on 28 June 1950, there was a massacre at Seoul National University Hospital during the First Battle of Seoul in which between 700 and 900 medical personnel and patients were shot or buried alive.

Republic of Korea troops were responsible for massacring 719 unarmed civilians in Geochang, South Korea, between 9 and 11 February 1951. Amongst the victims were 385 children. The same division, the 11th, had carried out a massacre at Sancheong-Hamyang, in which 705 civilians, 85 per cent of whom were women, children and the elderly, just a few days earlier. The first person to report the massacre to the National Assembly, a Geochang assemblyman, was sentenced to death but a second investigation in May 1951 uncovered the involvement of ROK troops. Two officers were sentenced to life imprisonment but clemency was granted by President Rhee to other perpetrators.

The North Koreans, of course, were also responsible for some atrocities. On 17 August 1950, 41 United States Army prisoners of war were shot dead by troops of the NKPA on Hill 303, above Waegwan in South Korea, during the Battle of the Pusan Perimeter. The soldiers – mortar operators – were taken captive after North Korean troops surrounded troops of the 2nd Battalion, 5th Cavalry Regiment, 1st Cavalry Division as they crossed the Naktong River at Hill 303. Most of their fellow soldiers managed to escape but the mortar operators were taken after they misidentified the North Korean troops as South Korean. The North Koreans attempted to move their prisoners back across the river and out of the battle but were subject to a heavy counter-attack. As American forces began to make ground, the NKPA started to retreat and, as they did so, an officer ordered that the prisoners be shot as they would slow them down. This act provoked outrage from the Americans who dropped leaflets from planes onto North Korean lines demanding that the officers responsible be held accountable for the atrocity. Concerned at the way POWs were being treated by their men, the NKPA leaders instituted stricter regulations as to the treatment of prisoners.

There were many more massacres, such as the one at 'Bloody Gulch', west of Masan in South Korea where the NKPA executed 75 US Army prisoners; at Ganghwa County in Inchon, South Korean forces killed between 212 and 1,300 civilians accused of collaboration between 6 and 9 January 1951; on July 16 1950, 30 unarmed and critically wounded US soldiers and a chaplain were cut off and massacred by North Korean troops on a mountain above the village of Tuman in South Korea; and South Korean police executed more than 460 civilians, including at least 23 children under the age of 10 at Namyangju in the Gyeonggi-do district of north-western South Korea. In 2008, trenches were found containing the bodies of children in Daejon, South Korea and in other places. All had been executed and photographs once again confirmed that the American authorities were aware of such atrocities at the time.

In 2005, the South Korean government created the Truth and Reconciliation Commission (South Korea) to investigate incidents in Korean history which occurred from the time of Japanese rule in Korea, starting in 1910, through to the end of authoritarian rule in the country with the election of President Kim Young-sam in 1993. Amongst atrocities investigated by the commission are many that took place during the Korean War. It estimates that tens of thousands of people were executed in 1950, during the first summer of the conflict.

The entire Korean peninsula had been devastated by the three years of warfare. There had been destruction, millions of deaths, and many were gravely wounded or missing. Families were separated and communities were shattered. The extent of the poverty that existed as a result of the war was staggering and there was an appalling amount of suffering. It looked as if it would take many years for each side to recover, if at all. Anyone thinking that, however, underestimated the determination, resilience and commitment of the people of this, at the time, embattled peninsula. Their leaders, too, must take a great deal of credit for what followed, because in the coming decades these formerly warring states developed into stable and strong entities with bold, if hard, leaders.

Postscript

The Republic of Korea

In South Korea Syngman Rhee resigned the presidency in 1960 as a result of a student uprising – the 'April 19 Revolution'. The country had struggled to rebuild and was reliant on aid from the United States. Rhee had been re-elected in 1956 for what should, according to the existing constitution, have been his second and final term, but as soon as he was in office, he changed that stipulation to permit a president to serve an unlimited number of terms. In 1960, at the age of 84, he won a fourth term in office, taking 90 per cent of the vote. It was not difficult for him to win this one because his opponent died a month before the election. The ensuing election for Vice President was judged by many to have been rigged in favour of Rhee's candidate which drove people to rise up. When police opened fire on demonstrators, Rhee's presidency was over. As protesters approached his residence on 28 April, the CIA flew him out of the country and, until his death in 1965, he lived in exile in Honolulu, Hawaii.

Thirteen months of instability followed Rhee's resignation but on 16 May 1961, the country underwent a military coup, led by General Park Chung-hee (1917-79). General Park had commanded the II and III Artillery Corps during the war and, by its end in 1953, had risen to the rank of Brigadier General. His period in office, which lasted 18 years from 1961 until 1979, was marked by political repression and rapid economic growth. Often described as a ruthless dictator, Park gave himself sweeping powers in 1972 and, like his predecessor, changed the constitution to allow a president to serve an unlimited number of six-year terms. However, there was significant export-led economic development and huge improvements in the country's infrastructure, with a nationwide motorway system and the construction of the Seoul Metropolitan Subway system in the capital. He was assassinated in October 1979 by his close associate, Kim Jae-gyu (1926-80), Director of the South Korean Intelligence Agency.

Months of political turmoil ensued until, on 12 December 1979, there was another military coup, led by General Chun Doo-hwan (b. 1931). On 17 May 1980, he became president, immediately declaring martial law across the country. Universities were closed and further restrictions were applied to the press. Demonstrations against his assumption of office were violently suppressed by the South Korean army and he led the country in a ruthless dictatorial regime until 1989 when publicity surrounding the death by torture of a student led to the creation of the June Democracy Movement. Chun's party, the Democratic Justice Party, which had begun to distance itself from the general's unpopular regime, announced an election which was won by the party's leader, Roh Tae-woo (b. 1932). The following year, Seoul was the host city for the Olympic Games which provided South Korea with a boost for its economy and for its image around the world.

Invited to become a member of the United Nations in 1991, South Korea took a huge step forward in 1997 with the election to the presidency of Kim Dae-jung (1924-2009). President Kim had eight years previously been a political prisoner who had been sentenced to death, although that sentence had later been commuted to exile. The new president introduced what he called his 'Sunshine Policy', officially known as 'The Reconciliation and Cooperation Policy Towards the North', designed to soften the North's attitude to South Korea. The policy brought greater cooperation between the two nations and led to summits in 2000, 2007 and 2018. There were joint business ventures and meetings between family members that the war had separated. In 2000, Kim was awarded the Nobel Peace Prize for his work for democracy and human rights both in his own country and East Asia. In 2002, another global event, the FIFA World Cup, hosted in conjunction with Japan, further boosted the image of South Korea.

In 2007, a conservative government was elected, with the former mayor of Seoul, Lee Myung-bak (b. 1941) as president but, in 2010, the old enmity with North Korea resurfaced with an escalation in the number of border incidents. The majority of them took place close to the Korean Demilitarised Zone or the Northern Limit Line, a disputed demarcation line in the Yellow Sea between the two states. In March, the ROK warship ROKS *Cheonan* was sunk – allegedly by a submarine of the North Korean navy – with the loss of all 46 sailors on board, and in November an artillery barrage was unleashed by North Korea on Yeonpyeong island which resulted in the deaths of four people. South Koreans were disappointed and angered by both their government's response to the attacks and the attitude of the global community to them. An official report by the United Nations refused to name North Korea as responsible for the sinking of the *Cheonan*.

In 2012, the first woman was elected president. Park Geun-hye (b. 1952) was the daughter of former President Park. However, she was removed from office in 2016 following a series of huge demonstrations after she and her government were accused of bribery, corruption and influence-peddling on behalf of businesswoman Choi Soon-sil (b. 1956). Park was sentenced to 30 years in prison and Choi to 20. Other officials of the government were also arrested and imprisoned.

The elections following the dismissal and imprisonment of President Park returned the former student activist and human rights lawyer Moon Jae-in (b. 1953) who took office in May 2017. His regime has seen improving relations with South Korea's northern neighbour, and the highly successful Winter Olympics in Pyeongchang.

The Democratic Republic of Korea

Although there was comparative peace following the signing of the armistice, there were many inflammatory incidents – abductions, border incidents and assassination attempts on South Korea's political leaders. In 1968, North Korean commandos tried to murder President Park Chung-hee in his residence, the Blue House, but were stopped at a checkpoint just outside the building; 26 South Koreans died and 66 were wounded in the ensuing firefight. Another attempt failed in 1974 and a bombing in Rangoon in 1983 during an official visit by President Chung killed 21, but left the president unharmed because his car was delayed in traffic. In 1983, tunnels were discovered under the Demilitarised Zone. In 1976, in an episode known as the 'Axe Murder Incident', two United States Army officers who were part of a work party detailed to cut down a poplar tree in the Joint Security Area in the DMZ at Panmunjom, were killed by North Korean soldiers wielding axes. The tree had apparently been planted by North Korean ruler, Kim Il-sung. Such incidents served only to increase the antipathy of the two nations towards each other and for almost two decades after the war they did not speak to one another.

In 1971, this changed, however, when secret, high-level contacts were established, resulting in the 4 July North–South Joint Statement. This established independence, peace and nation-wide unity as the three principles of unification. It was designed to improve relations between the two parts of Korea and to soften their attitudes towards one another. But by 1973, the talks had failed, and South Korea had decided that the two nations would be better off staying apart.

Kim Il-sung had remained at the helm of North Korea, despite efforts by the Soviets and the Chinese to depose him in 1956. All Chinese forces finally left the country in October 1958, the date marking the final independence of North Korea. The country remained closely aligned with the two major communist powers, however, Kim skilfully playing them off against each other when they began to drift apart, a process that took place between 1956 and 1966. North Korea was part of the Non-Aligned Movement, the forum of 120 developing world states that were not associated with or opposed to any major power bloc. Instead of Marxism, Maoism or capitalism, North Korea espoused Kim's theory of Juche which suggested that 'man is the master of his destiny', that the Korean people should act as if they were 'masters of the revolution and construction' and that a nation can achieve true socialism by making itself self-reliant and strong.

The North Korean people's commitment to their country can be seen in the fact that their hard work helped their country make a quick recovery from the war. In fact, by 1957, industrial production had attained the levels achieved in the year before the start of the war and, until the 1960s, economic growth outstripped that of the South. Indeed, until around 1976, North Korean GDP per capita equalled that of South Korea. Decline set in in the 1980s, a situation made even more serious by the disintegration of the USSR in 1991 and the complete and sudden cessation of all Soviet aid. The obvious place to turn was China, but the Chinese were unable to supply food aid in sufficient quantities.

By this time, Kim Il-sung's health was deteriorating and in 1992, his son, Kim Jong-il (1941-2011), began to assume some of his duties. Meanwhile, North Korea was in an impasse with the United States over its development of nuclear weapons. In the midst of this crisis, in 1994, Kim Il-sung died of a heart attack. Kim Jong-il announced three years of mourning before declaring himself to be his father's successor. The crisis was ended with the Agreed Framework, signed by the USA and North Korea in October 1994, with the objective of stopping the country's nuclear development and normalising relations with the United States. The agreement finally broke down in 2003. Meanwhile, Kim was also engaging with the South as part of its Sunshine Policy.

In the mid-1990s, North Korea's harvests were badly affected by flooding which led to serious food shortages and widespread famine, and damaged transport links.

By 1996, things had got so bad that the North Korean government accepted food aid from the United Nations. The famine, also known in North Korea as the Arduous March or the March of Suffering, lasted from 1994 to 1998, and hundreds of thousands are thought to have died from hunger. The United States Census Bureau has estimated that between 500,000 and 600,000 lost their lives in the famine. The words 'famine' and 'hunger' were banned because their use implied that the government had failed.

When George W Bush (b. 1946) became President of the United States in 2001, he decided to treat North Korea as a 'rogue state', rejecting South Korea's Sunshine Policy and the Agreed Framework, negotiated by his predecessor, President Bill Clinton (b. 1946). Often during Bush's presidency, he referred to what he described as the 'Axis of Evil' – Iran, Iraq and North Korea. This demonisation encouraged North Korea to redouble its efforts to develop a nuclear capability and, on 9 October 2006, it announced that it had staged its first test of a nuclear weapon. The next United States President, Barack Obama (b. 1961) instituted a new policy towards North Korea – 'strategic patience' – while the sinking of the *Cheonan* and other incidents perpetrated by the North Koreans increased tension.

Kim Jong-il died of a heart attack in December 2011 and was succeeded by his youngest son, Kim Jong-un (b. 1983) who was just 28 years old. At first it was assumed that his uncle, Jang Song-thaek (1946-2013) would take on a regency role as the new, young leader was too inexperienced. But, on 24 December 2011, Kim was publicly declared to be Supreme Commander of the Korean People's Army. The official newspaper of the Central Workers' Party of Korea, *Rodong Sinmun*, announced two days later that, since his father's death, Kim had been acting as chairman of the Central Military Commission and as supreme leader of North Korea. In the following March and April, he was elected to all of his father's old government positions. He made his first public speech on 15 April at the 100th anniversary parade celebrating his grandfather's birth. It was entitled 'Let Us March Forward Dynamically Towards Final Victory, Holding Higher the Banner of Songun'. 'Songun' is the 'military first' policy of North Korea. When, in July 2012, he was accorded the rank of wonsu (marshal) in the military he was confirmed as chief of the North Korean military.

Nowadays, Kim Jong-un is part of a triumvirate that heads the executive branch of the North Korean government. The other members are Premier Kim Jae-ryong (b. 1950) – no relation to Kim Jong-un – and the president of the North Korean parliament, Choe Ryong-hae (b. 1950). Kim Jong-un commands the armed forces, Kim Jae-ryong heads the government and handles domestic affairs, and Choe Ryong-hae handles foreign relations. But Kim Jong-un, like his father and grandfather before him, exercises absolute control over the government and the country.

Kim broke with tradition in 2014 by attending

a concert performed by the all-female pop band, Moranbong Band. He used this event to introduce his wife to the public, a step that was unprecedented for a North Korean leader. He also differed from his father by making a New Year's address in 2013, something his grandfather Kim Il-sung had done, but which his father, Kim Jong-il, never did in his 17 years as leader.

In 2013, Kim took steps to improve the economy with the 'Socialist Corporate Responsible Management System'. These measures sought to give enterprises increased autonomy. Measures were also taken to increase productivity on collective farms. The ultimate aim was to improve living standards and to increase the availability of goods made in North Korea as well as to provide a boost for international trade. A construction boom has been taking place in Pyongyang and amusement parks, water parks, a ski resort and even a dolphinarium have been built.

Alongside this, however, there has always been a darker side, and paranoia and suspicion have led to purges and executions. Jang Song-thaek, the uncle who had almost become regent, was accused of being a traitor in December 2013. He was arrested and executed by firing squad. It is also rumoured that many members of Jang's family have also been executed, even the children and grandchildren of close relatives. Korean state media announced on 12 December 2013 that the army 'will never pardon all those who disobey the order of the Supreme Commander'.

The North Koreans have also been accused of human rights violations. The United Nations Special Rapporteur, Marzuki Darusman (b. 1945), produced a report in which he claimed that Kim and other members of the North Korean government were accountable for crimes against humanity, recommending that Kim should be put on trial at the International Criminal Court. Meanwhile, the case of the American student Otto Warmbier (1994-2017) caused outrage in the United States and around the world. Warmbier, part of a guided tour group on a visit to North Korea, was accused in June 2017 of attempting to steal a propaganda poster from his hotel. He was sentenced to 15 years' imprisonment with hard labour, but, shortly after he was sentenced, he suffered a severe brain injury from an unknown cause and slipped into a coma. The authorities claimed it was as a result of botulism and a sleeping pill and when he was released after 17 months in captivity he was still in a comatose state. Taken back to America, he died six days later. A US Federal Court found the North Korean government liable for his death. US President Donald Trump (b. 1946) said that he believed the North Korean leader when he promised that Warmbier's death was nothing to do with him, but the dead student's parents criticised the president, accusing him of making excuses for Kim and what they termed 'his evil regime'.

Controversially, North Korea has maintained its programme of developing nuclear weapons. It conducted missile tests in 2013, 2016 and 2017 and has carried out more than 80 of them in total. It is believed that Kim sees nuclear capability as necessary for his country to deter attacks and it has been reported that he also views nuclear weapons as the guarantor of the survival of him and his regime.

It is estimated that North Korea possesses between 15 and 60 bombs, including hydrogen bombs, while its Hwasong-15 missile is capable of reaching any target in the United States. It has been subjected to sanctions by the United Nations for its continued determination to pursue the development of a nuclear capability and for its missile development programme.

When Donald Trump assumed the presidency of the United States at the start of 2017, a period of heightened tension began between America and North Korea. It started with a series of North Korean missile and nuclear tests that made it apparent that the country now had the ability to launch ballistic missiles that could travel beyond the surrounding region. It was also apparent that North Korea's nuclear development was moving faster than had previously been realised. Indeed, in September of that year, the North Koreans conducted their sixth test of a nuclear weapon. In April 2017, North Korea's deputy ambassador to the United Nations accused the United States of making the Korean peninsula once again 'the world's biggest hotspot'.

Meanwhile, the North Korean government announced 'its readiness to declare war on the United States if North Korean forces were to be attacked'. All of this followed the announcement by the US Navy that it was sending a navy strike group, headed by the USS *Carl Vinson* supercarrier, to the West Pacific. In error the naval operation was presented as being aimed at the Korean peninsula when, in reality, it was nowhere near. Part of the problem was that, following the concerns about the North Korean ballistic missile programme, President Donald Trump had announced on 17 April: 'We are sending an armada.' Ramping the tension up even further was a joint American and South Korean military exercise in August 2017, coupled with repeated American threats. The rhetoric increased and there were grave concerns about a possible war, especially when Kim threatened Australia with nuclear weapons because he claimed that they were taking the side of the Americans. Trump, again in April, said in a speech: '[t]here is a chance that we could end up having a major, major conflict in North Korea'. In September, in a speech at the United Nations, President Trump famously dubbed Kim 'Rocket Man'. He said:

'If it is forced to defend itself or its allies, we will have no choice but to totally destroy North Korea. "Rocket Man" is on a suicide mission for him and his regime. The United States are ready, willing and able, but hopefully this will not be necessary.'

Trump also criticised China for supporting North Korea, describing it as 'an outrage that some nations would arm, supply and financially support a country that imperils the world with nuclear conflict'. He increased sanctions against North Korea with legislation targeted at businesses and financial institutions that were engaged in business with the country.

Kim responded to Trump's jibes two days after the UN speech, calling the US president 'a mentally deranged US dotard' and vowing that his nation would deliver the 'highest level of hard-line countermeasure in history'. His foreign minister described Trump as a 'barking dog'. He hinted that North Korea might be considering the largest-ever test of a hydrogen bomb in the Pacific Ocean. This would have been the first atmospheric nuclear test since a Chinese one in 1980. By the end of the month, however, the two countries were talking to each other and the US Secretary of State, Rex Tillerson (b. 1952), announced that they were discussing the possibility of direct talks. Nonetheless, in November, North Korea conducted its third intercontinental ballistic missile test.

Tensions eased considerably at the beginning of the following year and suddenly North Korea announced the restoration of the Seoul–Pyongyang hotline which had been out of use for the previous two years. The softening of the North Korean attitude to its southern neighbour became apparent when, in his New Year Speech, the North Korean leader announced that he was open to discussing with South Korea participation in the forthcoming Winter Olympic Games which were being staged in the South. Consequently, North and South

Korea marched together at the opening ceremony for the games and the women's ice hockey team contained players from both nations. The North's delegation to the games included Kim's sister, Kim Yo-jong (b. 1988).

In the following months there was frantic diplomatic activity and North Korea suspended its nuclear and missile tests. President Moon and Kim Jong-un finally met at the Joint Security Area at Panmunjom on 27 April 2018, Kim crossing the MDL, signalling the first time that a North Korean leader had done so. They signed the Panmunjom Declaration in which they both agreed to cooperate on officially ending the Korean War. They also agreed to 'make active efforts to seek the support and cooperation of the international community for the denuclearization of the Korean peninsula'.

It had suddenly been announced on 8 March that Donald Trump and Kim Jong-un would meet, but Trump abruptly cancelled the meeting on 24 May, due to the 'tremendous anger and open hostility' that the North Korean leader had displayed towards him and the United States. A week later, in characteristic style, he reversed the decision and the two finally shook hands on 12 June in Singapore. The result of their apparently amicable talks was a joint statement that read:

1. The United States and the DPRK commit to establish new United States-Democratic People's Republic of Korea relations in accordance with the desire of the peoples of the two countries for peace and prosperity.

2. The United States and the Democratic People's Republic of Korea will join their efforts to build a lasting and stable peace regime on the Korean Peninsula.

3. Reaffirming the April 27 2018 Panmunjom Declaration, the Democratic People's Republic of Korea commits to work towards the complete denuclearization of the Korean Peninsula.

4. The United States and the Democratic People's Republic of Korea commit to recovering Prisoner of War/Missing in Action remains, including the immediate repatriation of those already identified.

Suspicions remained, and it was reported on various news outlets, that North Korea was continuing production of enriched uranium for nuclear weapons and that it had a number of secret nuclear sites. President Trump said that he believed they had stopped nuclear testing and that he was not imposing a timeline on total denuclearisation. However, sanctions would remain firmly in place until denuclearisation was complete.

A second summit between the two leaders was held in Hanoi on 28–29 February 2019, a meeting cut short without agreement, however because, President Trump said, North Korea wanted an end to all sanctions. The North Korean Foreign Minister, Ri Yong-ho (b. 1956), however, stated in a rare press conference that North Korea had sought only a partial lifting of sanctions.

On 12 June, President Trump described a letter he

had received from Kim Jong-un as 'beautiful'. And on 26 June it was announced that there were talks ongoing about a third summit between the two leaders. A photo was later issued by the North Korean government of Kim reading a letter from Donald Trump which he described as 'excellent'. Unfortunately, however, the North Korean leader then denied the reports of talks with the United States and insisted that relations remained hostile with the American State Department. Nonetheless, the two did meet again, at the Demilitarised Zone at Panmunjom, and Trump became the first US president to set foot on North Korean soil. They joined South Korean President Moon Jae-in for discussions and agreed once more to work towards denuclearisation.

Bibliography

Cumings, Bruce, *The Korean War*, New York, Modern Library reprint edition 2011

Halberstam, David, *The Coldest Winter: America and the Korean War*, New York, Hyperion 2007

Halliday, Jon and Cumings, Bruce, *Korea: The Unknown War*, New York, Viking 1988

Hastings, Max, *The Korean War*, London, Simon & Schuster 1988

Lowe, Peter, *The Korean War*, London, Macmillan Press 2000

Rees, David, *Korea: The Limited War*, Baltimore, Penguin Books 1964

Stokesbury, James L., *A Short History of the Korean War*, New York, Harper Perennial 1990

Stueck Jr., William, *The Korean War: An International History*, Princeton, Princeton University Press 1977

Tucker, Spencer T (editor), *Encyclopedia of the Korean War* (3 Volumes), Santa Barbara, ABC-CLIO 2000

Index